THE DISCIPLINE
OF SUBJECTIVITY

THE DISCIPLINE
OF SUBJECTIVITY:
AN ESSAY ON MONTAIGNE

ERMANNO BENCIVENGA

PRINCETON UNIVERSITY PRESS
Princeton, New Jersey

Copyright © 1990 by Princeton University Press
Published by Princeton University Press,
41 William Street,
Princeton, New Jersey 08540
In the United Kingdom: Princeton University Press, Oxford

Library of Congress Cataloging-in-Publication Data

Bencivenga, Ermanno, 1950-
The discipline of subjectivity : an essay on Montaigne
Ermanno Bencivenga.
p. cm.
Includes bibliographical references.
ISBN 0-691-07364-3 (alk. paper)
1. Montaigne, Michel de, 1533-1592. I. Title.
B785.M74B46 1990
194—dc20   89-36306

Publication of this book has been aided by the Whitney Darrow
Publication Reserve Fund of Princeton University Press

This book has been composed in Linotron Bembo

Princeton University Press books are printed on acid-free paper,
and meet the guidelines for permanence and durability of the
Committee on Production Guidelines and Book Longevity of the
Council of Library Resources

Printed in the United States of America
by Princeton University Press,
Princeton, New Jersey

10 9 8 7 6 5 4 3 2

*To Ben and Gerry and Karin
and Leslie and Rob and Sally
and all other parts of myself*

CONTENTS

PREFACE

I HAVE WRITTEN books with long bibliographies, but such books age fast; so when I felt I was ready for it I wrote this book, which has a very short bibliography. Of course, the things I've written here have been written many times before, but I had to write them again, my way. Those things were missing from my life, and I wrote them in order to find them. Now they have a place in my life, though tomorrow never knows: what one no longer misses, is already about to be lost.

Padua, June 1989

A NOTE ON TEXTS

UNLESS OTHERWISE indicated, all Montaigne quotes in this book are taken from the English edition of the *Complete Works*, translated by Donald M. Frame (Stanford, Calif.: Stanford University Press, 1957). In the references to the *Essays*, the roman numeral refers to the book and the arabic numeral to the essay; "*Letter n*" refers to the *n*th letter. I have not italicized Montaigne's quotes from other authors, limiting myself to citing those authors. Occasionally, I have also used the French *Oeuvres complètes*, text established by A. Thibaudet and M. Rat, introduction and notes by M. Rat (Paris: Gallimard, Bibliothèque de la Pléiade, 1962). Finally, since this book is intended to be a direct dialogue with Montaigne's text, most other references are to my own work. Complete bibliographical information can be found at the back of the book.

THE DISCIPLINE
OF SUBJECTIVITY

Volventi mihi multa ac varia mecum diu, ac per multos
dies sedulo quaerenti memetipsum ac bonum meum,
quidve mali evitandum esset; ait mihi subito, sive ego
ipse, sive alius quis extrinsecus, sive intrinsecus, nescio;
nam hoc ipsum est quod magnopere scire molior.
—Augustine, *Soliloquiorum Libri Duo*, I 1

Whether I shall turn out to be the hero of my own life,
or whether that station will be held by anybody else,
these pages must show.
—Charles Dickens, *David Copperfield*, Chapter 1

CHAPTER ONE

I SEARCH

I do not find myself in the place where I look; and I
find myself more by chance encounter than by
searching my judgment.

(*I 10, pp. 26–27*)

≥♣

The Objective

DO I EXIST? Of course I do. An unknown, almighty power could
well annihilate the whole world around me (and perhaps already
did), but there is something it cannot do: it cannot annihilate me so
long as I am a terrified spectator of its incinerating action, or so long
as I wonder whether such an action has taken place or not. *My* puz-
zlement, or *my* terror, is conclusive evidence that I, at least, have
not been incinerated yet.

Do I know something about myself? Of course I do. I may be
wrong about this being a crazy spring day, with the sun fighting to
come out but being repeatedly chased and suffocated by black,
thundering clouds. I may be wrong about there being a screen in
front of me, and about green impalpable letters being plotted on it
by the pressure of my fingers on the keys. And I may be wrong
about these being fingers, or their being mine. I can imagine situations in which none of these beliefs are true. But no situation can be
imagined in which it is false that I *see* black thundering clouds, or
green impalpable letters, or that I feel pressure *as if* I had fingers and

they were hitting keys. This knowledge cannot be denied; in fact, it cannot even be perfected. Not only is it the rock bottom of what I know, it is also top quality as far as what I *can* know.

Do I have, to some extent, control over myself? Of course I do. A threatening, hostile environment often makes it impossible for me to pursue my plans, or even forces me into outcomes I will hate and regret; but this unfortunate consequence of my finitude and limitations does not cancel the fact that I, too, am a party in the transaction, an *acting* party, a party with a will of its own. If worst comes to worst, and the environment becomes too hostile and threatening, I can always retreat into myself, refuse to impose my power over fortune and external things, and rest content with maintaining my independence of judgment. Nobody but I can take that away from me; even the sweeping passions that occasionally win me over would not have their way if I did not let them, that is, if I did not—perhaps half-mindedly, perhaps discontentedly—*decide* to let them. The world is not my own, but I most certainly am.

Or am I?

Early in the *Meditations*, Descartes reaches a view of the self much like the one sketched above. The self is absolutely certain of its own existence, absolutely certain of its nature, which is that of a thinking thing (and remains untouched by the reality or unreality of *what* is being thought), and can acquire maximum control over itself by minimizing the intervention of external agencies, that is, by withdrawing to a small, quiet corner of the earth and refusing to take part in anything but the search after (its own) truth. The self is absolute transparency: what is opaque in its perception of itself is due to the Other, and though there may have to be an Other given that *this* self is not infinite, leaving that Other—at least temporarily—on the side will allow the self to recover its primordial, immediate, and unquestionably veridical relation with itself. On the basis of this recovery, it will be possible to return to the Other, and to account for it in an effective, indeed conclusive, way. Thus in Descartes's view, (the thought of) subjectivity is the only safe way to begin a rational reconstruction of the world—a position that, extreme as it is, is also quite popular, to the point of being commonsensical, among scholars and laymen alike.[1]

There is also another, more elaborate, extreme in this matter, typified by Kant. It intimates that only *spatio*-temporal objects can be assumed to exist, and hence that the presence revealed by self-consciousness must be provided with hands and feet before we can attempt to predicate being of it. In fact, it even suggests that Descartes's may be the wrong order of business: you don't first assert the existence of something and *then* ask what it is. The existence of something becomes an issue only *after* it has been decided what that something is: "The category [of existence] as such does not apply to an indeterminately given object but only to one of which we have a concept and about which we seek to know whether it does or does not exist outside the concept" (*Critique of Pure Reason*, B423 footnote). And, finally, this position acknowledges that the will and its free agency must be postulated, but denies that such postulation accounts for much; rather, what is reached through it is the limit of explanation, something that cannot be avoided but cannot be understood, either. To say that an event occurs because I want it to occur—that is, to locate in my free choice the *origin* of the event—is tantamount to saying that I don't know *why* the event occurred. A reference to freedom may be an effective question stopper, but not one that brings with it real enlightenment.

Of these two extremes, I feel closer to the latter, and elsewhere I have tried to make some sense of it,[2] though with more sympathy for making waves and bringing out the underlying tensions than its official champions are likely to reveal. But it is time to go beyond programmatic and general statements about what is and what is not possible, what is and what is not knowledge, what is and what is not an object, and turn our attention to some of the details of the matter. Our relation to the self may be essentially different from our

---

[1] Which does not exclude that, when laymen come to appreciate the consequences of this position, they may have second thoughts about it. More about this later.

[2] See my *Kant's Copernican Revolution*.

relation to anything else; it may be noncognitive, and may even be a delusion. Accepting these negative statements, however, is not an end but a beginning: the beginning of an investigation of what exactly the structure of the relation—or of the delusion—is.

In carrying out this investigation, I found it useful to follow the devious and occasionally disconcerting paths traced by an author who was dead long before Descartes and Kant made their statements, and who has been all but conspicuously absent from Anglo-American philosophical reflection: Michel de Montaigne. Several times in his *Essays*, Montaigne makes the point (to which I will return) that he never erases something he wrote earlier because he does "not always find again the sense of [his] first thought; [he does] not know what [he] meant to say, and often [gets] burned by correcting and putting in a new meaning, because [he has] lost the first one, which was better" (II 12, pp. 425–26). Mankind, or our culture, has no better (collective) memory than Montaigne attributes to himself; it is true of it, too, that because something comes later it is not necessarily better, or wiser. Perhaps we have lost the first meaning, and degenerated as a result. Perhaps we need to recover that earlier meaning. My going back to Montaigne is an attempt at such recovery.

Montaigne's declared purpose is that of studying himself:

> The world always looks straight ahead; as for me, I turn my gaze inward, I fix it there and keep it busy. Everyone looks in front of him; as for me, I look inside of me; I have no business but with myself; I continually observe myself, I take stock of myself, I taste myself. Others always go elsewhere . . . ; as for me, I roll about in myself. (II 17, p. 499)

> I study myself more than any other subject. That is my metaphysics, that is my physics. (III 13, p. 821)[3]

And he considers it both a duty and a pleasure to give a faithful account of his findings:

---

[3] See also II 12, p. 425; III 5, pp. 643–44.

I owe a complete portrait of myself to the public. (III 5, p. 677)

I take such great pleasure in being judged and known that it is virtually indifferent to me in which of the two forms I am so. (III 8, p. 705)

This account—this "confession" (II 17, p. 495)[4]—is the very text of the *Essays*: "I am myself the matter of my book," Montaigne writes, and "you would be unreasonable to spend your leisure on so frivolous and vain a subject" (*To the Reader*, p. 2). But *we* do not consider the subject either frivolous or vain; on the contrary, this thorough examination of a self can provide us with an illuminating example of how to search, and perhaps find, the difference, and the relation, between the I and the Other. This example we must savor and cherish, much more than the vacuous generalities philosophers usually regale us with; after all, we are creatures who tend to "adjust themselves not to reason but to example" (III 6, p. 689),[5] and hence example is for us the best means of instruction.

I would have told my master home truths, and watched over his conduct, if he had been willing. Not in general, by school-masterly lessons, which I do not know—and I see no true reform spring from them in those who know them—but by observing his conduct step by step, at every opportunity, judging it with my own eyes, piece by piece, simply and naturally. (III 13, p. 825)[6]

The Truth about the Self

Montaigne claims to have complete control over the matter he treats. "[N]o man," he says, "ever treated a subject he knew and

---

[4] See also III 5, p. 643: "I confess myself in public."

[5] The immediate reference of this quote is to those subjects who are spoiled by a liberal king. But we will see in footnote 2 of Chapter 5 that this case is a crucial one, since it is paradigmatic (according to Montaigne) of the way in which human needs evolve, and hence also of how men "adjust themselves" in a changing environment.

[6] For more details about this contrast between the generalities of philosophy and concrete, empirical reality, see the section on *Discipline* later in this chapter.

understood better than I do the subject I have undertaken" (III 2, p. 611). The reason is that his subject is himself, and "there is no witness so sure as each man to himself" (II 16, p. 474). "There is no one but yourself who knows whether you are cowardly and cruel, or loyal and devout. Others do not see you, they guess at you by uncertain conjectures. . . . Therefore do not cling to their judgment; cling to your own" (III 2, p. 613). Besides, he is "a sworn enemy of any falsification" (I 40, p. 186) and "singularly scrupulous about lying" (III 11, p. 786),[7] and has "a mortal fear of being taken to be other than [he is] by those who come to know [his] name" (III 5, p. 643). The obvious conclusion of all these premises is that his book contains the truth about him, what a man who did not meet him could only have gained by "long acquaintance and familiarity . . . , and more surely and exactly" (III 9, p. 750), and leaves nothing about him "to be desired or guessed" (ibid., p. 751).

So far, Montaigne's statements sound very Cartesian. He may have devoted more time, energy, and single-minded attention to the exploration of his own self, and consequently may have come to know more details about it, but the general story he tells seems consistent with the basic tenets of subjectivism. To dispel this appearance, we need to explore a little further.

A first element that gives us pause here is the claim, repeated several times in the *Essays*, that Montaigne is trying "not to establish the truth but to seek it" (I 56, p. 229). In line with this aim, he describes his methodology as proceeding by trial and error, by testing things, *essaying* them,[8] taking them "from some unaccustomed

---

[7] Emphasis on the importance of truth and truth-telling is common throughout the *Essays*. Thus, because "[t]ruth is the first and fundamental part of virtue," and "[w]e must love it for itself" (II 17, p. 491), Montaigne declares that "cost [him] what it may, [he is] determined to tell the facts" (ibid., p. 500; see also III 10, p. 780), that he "admit[s] the truth when it hurts [him], just as when it serves [him]" (III 5, p. 675) and "would rather fail in [his] mission than fail to be true to [him]self" (III 1, p. 600), that he "give[s] a warm welcome to truth in whatever hand [he] find[s] it" (III 8, p. 705), and that one "must pass over [the] common rules of civility in favor of truth and liberty" (ibid., p. 720).

[8] See, for example, I 26, p. 107 ("As for the natural faculties that are in me, of which this book is the essay"); II 17, p. 495 ("my judgment . . . , of which these are the essays"), as well as the next quote set off in the main text. Incidentally, it is ironic

point of view . . . [s]cattering a word here, there another, samples
separated from their context, dispersed, without a plan and without
a promise" (I 50, p. 219). The result of this activity, which he considers not his "teaching, but [his] study" (II 6, p. 272), is sometimes
described in very negative terms:

> In fine, all this fricassee that I am scribbling here is nothing
> but a record of the essays of my life, which, for spiritual
> health, is exemplary enough if you take its instruction in re-
> verse. (III 13, p. 826)

> [T]he more I frequent myself and know myself, the more my
> deformity astonishes me, and the less I understand myself. (III
> 11, p. 787)

These passages are quite inconsistent with the picture of an expert
who masters the "essence" of his subject (in this case, himself; see II
6, p. 274) and provides a reliable report on it. What they suggest
instead is a "rambling" procedure (see III 6, p. 692) which, if it ever
gets anywhere, only does so because "who is there who, shooting
all day, will not sometime hit the mark?" (I 11, p. 29; quoted from
Cicero). Perhaps the specific subject Montaigne is interested in is
responsible for this outcome, since "[i]f others examined themselves attentively, as I do, they would find themselves, as I do, full
of inanity and nonsense. Get rid of it I cannot without getting rid of
myself" (III 9, p. 766). But still, an inconsistency is there and some
assessment of it is needed. Shall we blame it on Montaigne's care-
free attitude, or rather take it as a sign that something is amiss in the
superficial interpretation we have developed so far? An answer to
this question will come by a relatively tortuous route.

First of all, we saw that Montaigne is an "enemy of any falsifica-

---

to see how far the original meaning of the word "essay" (French: *essay*)—and the one
relevant to Montaigne—has now been perverted, to the point of being turned into
its opposite. What was once a test, a try, a leap in the dark has now become the
considered statement of solid, established results. This "concretion" movement is the
outcome of important forces, not unconnected with the issues discussed here, and as
such will surface again in what follows—specifically, within the discussion conducted in Chapter 6 of how the "game" of philosophy becomes an institution.

tion." It is natural to read this statement as meaning that he is averse to providing the wrong *description* of anything—including himself. But this reading has an important presupposition: what is to be described must be ontologically prior to (and hence, independent of) the activity of describing it. Unless describing is limited to reproducing, and an original is invoked as the standard for accuracy, one cannot make sense of the claim that the description is correct, or incorrect. Thus, if I say that it is wrong to describe the table out there as blue, I am presupposing that there would be a table out there, and one that is, for example, brown, even if I did not speak, or for that matter even if, instead of speaking, I ceased altogether to exist. What I say is entirely irrelevant to the being and nature of the table, which would continue to be itself, and to be brown, and to be not blue, whatever accurate or inaccurate description of it I or anybody else uttered.

In the case of the self, however, it is suggested over and over in the *Essays* that the search for it and the attempt at characterizing it (as conducted in the book) are at least in a relation of mutual determination with the object of the search, that is, that the search is also a *constitution* of the self:

> In modeling this figure upon myself, I have had to fashion and compose myself so often to bring myself out, that the model itself has to some extent grown firm and taken shape. . . . I have no more made [*faict*] my book than my book has made me. (II 18, p. 504)

Clearly, this statement is not unquestionable, and later it will be questioned.[9] But proceeding one step at a time, it is useful to emphasize here that the statement is directly opposed to the presupposition above, and to the reading based upon it. If the book made Montaigne at least as much as he made the book, then Montaigne and the book are ontologically interdependent: a different book would have made a different Montaigne, of whom different descriptions would have been true or false. So the statements con-

[9] See below, pp. 13–15.

tained in the book itself—in what sense can *they* be true or false of Montaigne? And how are we to understand his aversion to falsification in the case of the self, where there is nothing (ontologically) prior to his report for him to report about?

"We are men," Montaigne says elsewhere, "and hold together, only by our word" (I 9, p. 23). There are two ways in which "our word" is crucial for maintaining social cohesion, and both of them figure prominently in the essay in which this statement occurs. One is when we describe something that already is the case, and others are to take "our word" for it; call this the *descriptive* use of words. The other is when we commit ourselves to doing something, and give "our word" that we will do it; call this the *self-prescriptive* use of words.[10] In both cases there is ample room for falsification, though of a different nature: when words are used descriptively it results in lying, when they are used self-prescriptively it results in breaking promises. We know by now that in the case of the self, on the basis of what Montaigne says, the first kind of falsification is out of the question; but it is still possible that the second kind will turn out to be applicable, and that it will be the one he is primarily worried about.

In the essay "Of Vanity," we find the following remarks: "[I]n undertakings in which I am alone concerned and wholly free, if I say what I plan to do, it seems to me that I prescribe it for myself, and that to give knowledge of it to another is to impose it upon myself. It seems to me that I promise it when I mention it" (III 9,

[10] These two uses (which are clearly reminiscent of Austin's "locutionary" and "illocutionary" acts) are more interconnected (as, for that matter, are Austin's notions) than the present typology may suggest. On the one hand, words are used descriptively within the scope of a general (social) commitment to truthfulness (a commitment that Montaigne takes very seriously, to the point of judging as binding even promises extracted by the use of force—see III 1, p. 608), and on the other, their self-prescriptive use may be taken as descriptive of the *intentions* of the speaker (so that, if he breaks his commitment, he misdescribed those intentions). These interconnections can be used to analyze one concept in terms of the other (specifically, the practical notion of commitment in terms of the theoretical notion of accuracy, or vice versa), and some of the moves discussed below will have the effect of making us favor one such line (the second one). But for the moment it is in the interest of clarity to insist on the opposition.

p. 738). But to write his book would seem to be a typical case of an undertaking in which he is alone concerned and wholly free, so it is not surprising to find him say, later in the same essay:

> I feel this unexpected profit from the publication of my behavior, that to some extent it serves me as a rule. Sometimes there comes to me a feeling that I should not betray the story of my life. This public declaration obliges me to keep on my path, and not to give the lie to the picture of my qualities. (Ibid., p. 749)

We are now in a position to address the charge of inconsistency brought out earlier. It is in fact legitimate for Montaigne to claim, at the same time, that what he tells is the truth about himself and that there is no truth of the matter before the telling. The reason this strange conjunction of claims is legitimate is that the truth mobilized here is of a prescriptive nature. The book, primarily in its quality as a public object, imposes a commitment on the part of the self, and being an enemy to falsification in this context is being averse to breaking that commitment.[11] It is not so much that the book tells what the self is like; it is rather that the book tells the self what it is to be. Which, of course, does not mean that truth collapses into arbitrariness: making a decision about what to do next may be arbitrary to a point, but sticking to it certainly is not. The book forces consistency on the self, and hence ultimately forces it to *be*, since to be is to be one way rather than another. It is in this prescriptive sense that book and self come virtually to coincide, and Montaigne can say: "[W]e go hand in hand and at the same pace, my book and I" (III 2, pp. 611–12), and "[e]veryone recognizes me in my book, and my book in me" (III 5, p. 667). The book is the record of what the self has decided about itself, but also a record of decisions that come

---

[11] Superficially, we might justify this commitment on the basis of social conventions and practice, for "one must spruce up, . . . one must present oneself in an orderly arrangement, if one would go out in public" (II 6, p. 273). But later we will see that there is an important "theoretical" rationale for this practice: what is public coincides with what *is*, whereas the private—the "inside," the alleged originator (for the Cartesian) of our true being—is but a reaction to the very project of being *anything*.

to being by being written. And though this account will have to be supplemented, complicated, and partly contradicted later,[12] it is as much of an account as I can give at the moment.

Discipline

Thus Montaigne can claim consistently that he knows himself as well as anybody ever knew any subject, *and* that the search for the self conducted in his book is also a constitution, a making (*faire*), of the self, outside of which there is nothing definite, nothing to report about. But the latter statement, as I have said, is still far from unquestionable; in fact, the Cartesian would certainly object to it.[13] To some extent neither party can, or should, argue the other out of business. Open competition is here the best course; at the end of the present articulation of the consequences of one perspective—at the end of this book—the reader will decide whether to buy it or go elsewhere. But before getting to the consequences, it may be useful to place the debate against a wider background.

It is a peculiar attitude toward the subject matter that is primarily responsible, in my opinion, for statements like the above—an attitude that is quite uncommon in philosophical circles. The philosopher's tendency is to simplify, to "abstract": traditionally, the very area in which he conducts his activity—the area of conceptual reflection—is conceived as the result of such an abstraction. In order to arrive at it, one must let go of "irrelevant" details and concentrate

---

[12] Such an articulation will be conducted throughout most of this book and will come to its clearest statement in the last chapter. At that point, I will also be in a position to explain why Montaigne is so negative about the outcome of this process of self-construction.

[13] Note that "the Cartesian" is a more stereotypical, uninteresting, and strategically useful entity than the actual Descartes. The latter is in fact much closer to the position I am in the process of articulating than I can explore here; the reader will find some gestures in this direction in my "Descartes, Dreaming, and Professor Wilson." But though there is more of Montaigne in Descartes than one might think, it is clearest and most profitable, from a theoretical point of view, to insist on the elements of contrast between them (on the contrast between Montaigne and Descartes *minus* Montaigne, as it were).

on the essentials. Consistent with this general inclination, the Cartesian dismisses most of what is ordinarily attributed to the self as not being "really" its own. The self has no body, does not move, and has no physical influence on other objects; none of this, at least, essentially. What is left as being necessarily identical with the self is a minute fraction of what the self is ordinarily taken to include—so minute that probably only a philosopher would judge *it* as relevant.[14]

Ultimately, this tendency is what makes philosophy look sterile, and suggests that it "sometimes lingers" on "sharp, insubstantial subtleties" (II 11, p. 313)—those "frivolous subtleties" that we should "skip over" (I 20, p. 56; quoted from Seneca)—since by deleting and disregarding so much, one is likely to end up empty-handed. There is of course an alleged payoff: the simpler we make things, the easier it might seem to find the truth about them, and the more certain we might feel concerning our statements of such truth. And there is ample room for discussion of whether this payoff is delusive. Later, I will have something to contribute to this discussion; here I limit myself to pointing out that the tendency in question is not shared by Montaigne.

"Authors communicate with the people by some special extrinsic mark," we read in the *Essays*, "I am the first to do so by my entire being, as Michel de Montaigne, not as a grammarian or a poet or a jurist" (III 2, p. 611).[15] What this means, among other things, is that he is not going to simplify his charge and establish his own unity and consistency by restricting the range of himself.[16] Quite the contrary, he will spread himself out as far as he can, he will "speak of [him]self in different ways . . . because [he will] look at [him]self in different ways" (II 1, p. 242), and *then* only he will pose his major problem: how all this complex of things, attitudes, and actions, this

---

[14] See footnote 1 above.

[15] Which is just as well, considering how "comically" a teacher answered to one of Montaigne's men when asked who the gentleman following him was: "He is not a gentleman; he is a grammarian, and I am a logician" (I 26, p. 125).

[16] See II 32, p. 549: "[I]t is folly to try to judge by one feature things with so many aspects."

confused and confusing "patchwork," can be made to "stick" together,[17] how *one* individual can be personally responsible for all the
different and occasionally conflicting facets that cluster around any
human being. "[N]or do I think there is anything more arduous
than keeping oneself straight amid the waves and rush of the world,
loyally responding to and satisfying every part of one's charge" (II
33, p. 555).

It is from the point of view of this complexity that one can come
to appreciate, if not to share, Montaigne's belief that the unity and
consistency of the self is not an unquestionable starting point but
the (possible) result of an intense activity, that "[t]he greatest thing
in the world is to know how to belong to oneself" (I 39, p. 178),
and that more people should be able to say, as he (thinks he) is: "I
have put all my efforts into forming my life. That is my trade and
my work" (II 37, p. 596). For when we do not start with generalities, but consider what we in fact do (or think, or say), it is difficult
to deny that, on the surface at least, "[e]ach action plays its game
individually" (III 1, p. 601), and hence can hardly be "designate[d]
properly by some principal characteristic, so two-sided and motley
do they seem in different lights" (III 13, p. 825).

"I . . . go my way all in one piece," says Montaigne (III 2, p. 616),
and by now this proud statement of his is bound to appear even
prouder than the claim of complete mastery of his subject I quoted
earlier.[18] And we can also begin to articulate what is behind this
mastery and that coherence, what makes the difference between
them and the unconnected rambling they are always on the brink of
precipitating into: "In order to train my fancy even to dream with
some order and purpose, and in order to keep it from losing its way

---

[17] The terms "patchwork" (*lopins*) and "stick" (*attacher*) are Montaigne's. See II 1,
p. 244; I 26, p. 107.

[18] Consider the people to whom he is willing to attribute such consistency: Cato
the Younger, for example, one of those "heroic souls" whose "inimitable loftiness"
he does not "fail to observe" while "[c]rawling in the slime of the earth" (I 37, p.
169). Of him Montaigne says: "[H]e who has touched one chord of him has touched
all; he is a harmony of perfectly concordant sounds" (II 1, p. 241). In Chapter 2, the
issue of this "harmony" will come under closer investigation.

and roving with the wind, there is nothing like embodying and registering all the little thoughts that come to it" (II 18, p. 504).[19]

This important passage makes at least four points relevant to the present discussion: some of them are already known, one at least is new. First, it emphasizes that what we are up to is finding—in fact, tracing—our way, and keeping on it (that is, keeping consistent—"there are so few who have maintained the same will and the same pace in our public movements" [II 12, p. 323]). Second, it makes it clear that this way is not to be found by disregarding significant portions of our personality. It is easy to exclude something from sight by judging it unreal or unimportant—or "only a dream." Montaigne, however, is not going to be seduced by this simplistic strategy: in fact, he claims that "dreams are faithful interpreters of our inclinations [and] there is an art to sorting and understanding them" (III 13, p. 843). More generally, either the consistency is consistency of the whole or it is a delusion: in the words of Lucan quoted in the *Essays*, "[b]elieving nothing done while aught was left to do" (ibid., p. 854).

Third, we see from the above that the consistency of the whole self is to be obtained by paying careful attention to all the minute details of its behavior, that is, once again, not by applying ready-made rational principles but by carrying out a painstaking research of an *empirical* nature. Fourth, and most important here, we see also that this process must be a *training*. To *say* something is not enough, Montaigne insists in the *Essays*,[20] and, we may add, to *find* something is not enough either. What has been found once can be lost again, even if it is oneself. A "belly full of meat" does us no good "if it is not digested, if it is not transformed into us, if it does not make us bigger and stronger" (I 25, p. 101), and the same goes for

---

[19] The word translated here as "to train" is the French *renger*. Elsewhere in the Frame edition other words are also translated as "to train" (or its cognates): see, for example, I 23, p. 78 ("our most important training [*gouvernement*] is in the hands of nurses"); III 10, p. 780 ("What [the Stoics] did by virtue, I train myself [*je me duits*] to do by disposition"). See also II 37, p. 577, quoted on p. 116 below. (Incidentally, Montaigne's claim of being able to train himself to dream with order and purpose has some relevance to Descartes; see "Descartes, Dreaming, and Professor Wilson.")

[20] See II 3, p. 257; II 29, p. 536.

the tales we tell about what we are. We may enjoy the tales at the moment we tell them, but to make them become us we must tell them over and over again: we must use them (as an excuse) to exercise.

The importance of training and of its outcome, habit, will surface repeatedly in the following pages. For the moment, I am content to conclude this chapter with a simple statement, which justifies the title of the book. There needs to be discipline[21] for there to be a self. What exactly this discipline must accomplish we will have to explore, and our conclusions may startle some, but without a discipline that is intellectual and moral at the same time—since it involves both our notion of what we are and our sense of what we want—there would be nothing but a chaos of incoherent moves that send conflicting messages. Kant said something very important when he reminded us that the manifold of sensibility must be "gone through in a certain way, taken up, and connected" (*Critique of Pure Reason*, A77 B102) in order to be known; the main thing missing from this reminder is that it is not enough to complete the "synthesis" just once.

[21] This use of the word "discipline" is proper to Montaigne. See, for example, II 11, p. 313: "Socrates admitted . . . that that was in truth his natural propensity, but that he had corrected it by discipline [*discipline*]." See also III 6, p. 693; III 13, p. 823; ibid., p. 830 (quoted on p. 43 below, where Montaigne's conflicting values about discipline begin to emerge). Note also that Frame occasionally gives a different translation of the French word "*discipline*"; for example, at I 25, p. 105, he translates it as "teaching."

CHAPTER TWO

TRAINING

He must imbibe their ways of thinking, not learn
their precepts. And let him boldly forget, if he wants,
where he got them, but let him know how to make
them his own.

(I 26, p. 111)

❧

Memory

MONTAIGNE says that he has no memory. And he is talking about
no ordinary defect, no moderate nuisance; for once, his characterization of himself is conducted in quite emphatic terms.

There is no man who has less business talking about memory.
For I recognize almost no trace of it in me, and I do not think
there is another one in the world so monstrously deficient. All
my other faculties are low and common; but in this one I think
I am singular and very rare, and thereby worthy of gaining a
name and reputation. (I 9, p. 21)[1]

He hastens to add that lack of memory is not to be associated with
lack of judgment; quite the contrary, "excellent memories are prone
to be joined to feeble judgments" (ibid., p. 22). And he consoles
himself with various reasons: he remembers injuries less, he is less
inclined to lie, and he is less tormented by ambition. Still, the reader
is left with the impression that there is an objective lack here, and a

[1] For another equally strong (and more detailed) statement to the same effect, see
II 17, pp. 492–93.

deeply felt regret for it; after all, "Plato is right to call memory a great and powerful goddess" (ibid., pp. 21–22). But this impression is not accurate: though conceding, as is his wont, to traditional value judgments, Montaigne is working in fact to undercut them, or to change their meaning. Perhaps what he lacks is not so valuable, or perhaps he does not lack it, *when properly understood.*

All I know is myself, Montaigne says. Other things "will perhaps be known to me some day, or have been once, according as fortune may have brought me to the places where they were made clear. But I no longer remember them" (II 10, p. 296). Once again, this passage may be read as stating a peculiar feature of Montaigne the man—a feature that he refers to as having "no retentiveness" (ibid.). But it may also be read as suggesting a peculiar interpretation of what it is to know, or, for that matter, to remember—an interpretation according to which all *anybody* (not only Montaigne) *can* know, or remember, is oneself.

To clarify what I mean, I will proceed in two steps. I will introduce the first step by means of an example. Suppose that you ask me whether I know how to get to X, and I answer: "I am not sure. I have been there once, and then I found the way, but I can't say that I remember it. I will try." Then I sit in my car and I begin to drive. The first time I am offered the choice of turning right or left, I *feel* that I should go a certain way; the same feeling happens over and over again and guides me to my destination. As I proceed, I am not able to anticipate in thought—not to mention in speech—what my next move is going to be; nonetheless, as my moves follow one another, I become progressively more confident that I will get there, and eventually I do. If you now ask me to *explain* what I did, it may take a tremendous amount of concentration on my part to satisfy your request, possibly more concentration than I presently have, or will ever have, to offer. It is even possible that the next time I must take this trip, I will be just as uncertain that I can do it as I was now.

This example shows that there are two different ways in which one can be said to know, or remember, something. The typical object of the first kind of knowledge is a proposition: what you know in this sense is something you can *say* (or write). You can say that the sun is bright, or that the earth turns around it, and you may be able to quote from Newton's *Principia*; all these things, then—if you know them—you know propositionally. You know *that* the sun is bright, *that* the earth turns around it, and so on. The typical object of the second kind of knowledge, on the other hand, is a practice: what you know in this sense is something you can *do*.[2] You can walk, or swim, or recite the *Divine Comedy*;[3] all these things, then, you know practically. You know *how* to walk, *how* to swim, and so on.

Ideally, the two kinds of knowledge should go together. There may be a rudimentary, preliminary stage when one is not able to articulate one's own capacities in speech or thought, but then one gets to the point of really mastering the subject and the articulation comes as a matter of course. Which is just as well, you might say, since without this articulation knowledge and memory would seem to remain entirely private matters, and as such fall short of their most important function. For what is the value of knowing something if we cannot communicate it to others, and how can we communicate it without verbalizing it (and/or recording it in a book)? From the point of view of this ideal, my example refers precisely to the preliminary stage mentioned above: however much concentration it takes to express my presently mute feeling of how to get to X, that is the amount of concentration I must ask of myself. If I cannot attain it, then in fact I will not know—though mine was a promising case.

But perhaps this is the wrong ideal. Montaigne, at least, suggests that it is so. Specifically, he makes three relevant, and increasingly deviant, suggestions. First, he indicates that practical knowledge

---

[2] Of course, saying is also a doing of sorts, but still the first kind of knowledge does not reduce to a particular case of the second one. For what you know in the first sense is not *the saying*, but *the content* of what you say. This, at least, within the ideology where the first kind of knowledge holds its (privileged) place, whereas things become more complicated when the notion of content is called in question. See my "A New Paradigm of Meaning."

[3] Note that, since the *Divine Comedy* is not taken to have a truth-value, reciting it cannot be taken as (evidence of) knowledge in the first sense (whereas quoting from Newton's *Principia* can be taken as knowledge in both senses).

may be knowledge in its own right, and verbalization is not at all needed to perfect it. Possibly his clearest gesture in this direction is to be found in the passages where he attributes knowledge to animals, which are apparently excluded from any relation with propositions:

> [C]an birds use a square rather than a round figure, an obtuse rather than a right angle, without *knowing* their properties and their effects? . . . Do they shelter themselves from the rainy wind and face their dwelling toward the orient without *knowing* the different conditions of these winds . . . ? (II 12, p. 333; italics mine)

> Cranes, swallows, and other birds of passage, changing their residence according to the seasons of the year, show well enough the *knowledge* they have of their faculty of divination, and put it to use. (Ibid., p. 345; italics mine)

Nor will it do to claim that this knowledge of the animals is but "natural and obligatory instinct," since "[w]e must infer from like results like faculties, and consequently confess that this same reason, this same method that we have for working, is also that of the animals" (ibid., pp. 336–37). We must, then, share a "method for working" and some kind of (practical) reason with speechless swallows and cranes, whatever else propositional knowledge enables us to do.

Second, Montaigne suggests that verbalization is of no help for practical knowledge: knowing propositions about a practice is no guarantee that we master the practice. Neither "our pedants" nor "their students . . . are . . . nourished and fed with their learning . . . ; it passes from hand to hand for the sole purpose of making a show of it" (I 25, p. 100).[4] So when it comes to "the most useful

---

4 Several French words are translated as "learning" in the Frame edition; among them, *science* (in the preceding quote; in the next passage set off in the text we have instead the plural form *sciences*), *doctrine* (in the quote at the very end of this paragraph), and *sçavoir* (in the first quote of the next footnote). But all these words refer to a single constellation of traits, which includes being expressed in language, being recorded in books, being passed on by the schools, and being useless. A vivid ex-

teachings for the greatest and most necessary parts of our life" we see "these disciples, full of so much beautiful knowledge, obliged to imitate [the] stupid simplicity" of the "rustic, unpolished mob," or even to learn "from the very animals" (III 12, p. 803). It is indeed "a very great triumph for the honor of ignorance that knowledge herself throws us back into its arms when she finds herself powerless to strengthen us against the weight of ills" (II 12, p. 364). As for the promise that language could at least be used to *communicate* knowledge to others and instruct them, it is largely a delusion, at least as far as practices are concerned: to rehearse a point that was made earlier, and will surface again, the primary means of communication for practices is (practical) example.

> [S]ince it is a fact that learning . . . can only teach us *about* wisdom, integrity, and resolution, [the ancients] wanted to put their children from the first in contact with deeds, and instruct them, not by hearsay, but by the test of action . . . not only by precepts and words, but principally by examples and works. (I 25, p. 105)

Ultimately this means that, in *practice*, knowledge of propositions is useless: "We need hardly any learning to live at ease" (III 12, p. 794).

Third, Montaigne even insinuates that verbal, bookish learning is counterproductive. It "makes men's hearts soft and effeminate" (I 25, p. 106) and its carriers "unfit for social intercourse" (I 26, p. 121); it wastes energy and confers a false sense of security. The man of learning is nothing less than a con man:

> It seems to me that with this complication and interlacing of language . . . it turns out as with sleight-of-hand performers: their dexterity attacks and overpowers our senses, but it does

---

ample of this "learning complex" (to which the word "learning" will usually refer here) is given in the context of the first quote in the next paragraph (where, incidentally, Frame translates *sciences* as "knowledge"): "When the Goths ravaged Greece, what saved all the libraries from being set afire was that one of the invaders spread the opinion that this item might well be left intact to the enemy, to divert them from military exercises and keep them busy in sedentary and idle occupations" (I 25, p. 106).

not shake our belief at all. Aside from this legerdemain, they do nothing that is not commonplace and mean. For being more learned they are none the less inept. (III 8, p. 707)[5]

To summarize, one view of knowledge makes it consist of representing the world, and another makes it consist of coping with the world. And there is no doubt of where Montaigne's preference lies—though at this stage of the game his reasons for such preference may not be entirely transparent.[6]

[O]ur knowledge . . . is a miserable foundation for our rules and . . . is apt to represent to us a very false picture of things. (III 6, p. 693)

Note that the best managers are those who least know how to tell us how they are so, and that the self-satisfied storytellers most often do nothing worth while. (II 20, p. 512)

We are now ready for the second step of the argument. To begin, it is useful to return to my example once more. An interesting feature of the kind of "knowledge" I have of the way to X consists in the fact that I cannot establish any distance from what I know. If I could say, or write, or even think a set of propositions expressing this knowledge, then such utterances, or inscriptions, or mental occurrences would make the knowledge somewhat objective, that is, would make it a relation with something distinct from me, such that I can confront it, if need be, in a matter-of-fact way: take it or leave it, depending on where my interest lies. But since this distance cannot be established, what I know remains part and parcel of me,

---

[5] In the continuation of this passage, Montaigne claims to "love and honor learning as much as those who have it," and refers to a "true use" of it in which it is "man's most noble and powerful acquisition." What this true use comes down to, eventually, is as an excuse to practice: "It is my opinion that . . . Socrates argues more for the sake of the arguers than for the sake of the argument. . . . He takes hold of the first subject that comes along like a man who has a more useful aim than to illuminate it: to wit, to illuminate the minds that he undertakes to manage and exercise" (ibid., p. 708). Later in the book, I will focus on this gamelike, "experimental" aspect of language and learning.

[6] They will become clearer when we explore the ways of the mind, in Chapters 4–6.

in the precise sense that I cannot detach myself from it and operate with it at will: what I know is a system of automatic responses that I cannot help having when placed in the appropriate contexts.[7]

Now turn to Montaigne. In the essay "Our Feelings Reach Out beyond Us," he says: "We owe subjection and obedience equally to all kings, for that concerns their office; but we do not owe esteem, any more than affection, except to their virtue" (I 3, p. 9). But affection and esteem are personal sentiments, which relate us directly to the man behind the social mask. "If you press me to tell why I loved him," says Montaigne of his friend Etienne de La Boétie, "I feel that this cannot be expressed, except by answering: Because it was he, because it was I" (I 28, p. 139). So the conclusion follows that virtue is what is most proper to one, what can most properly be said to be *him*.

The next question to be asked is: When shall we attribute (a) virtue to a given man? And the answer, partially anticipated in the preceding chapter,[8] is that a single action is not enough: "When, though a coward against infamy, [a man] is firm against poverty; when, though weak against the surgeons' knives, he is steadfast against the enemy's swords, the action is praiseworthy, not the man" (II 1, p. 243).[9] One can force oneself to a number of praiseworthy moves, but the praise will not transfer from the moves to the person unless all of the moves show a consistency that is only possible when the whole has become automatic and the will, or the consciousness, has no longer anything to do with it:[10]

---

[7] Depending on the survival value of a given ability, the responses based on it may have more or less of an (immediate) impact on one's behavior. If you know how to swim, then you will be hard put *not* to make the appropriate movements upon being thrown into the water, whereas if you know how to get to X you will simply have an automatic sense of how to do it, but one that you might well not actualize even if there is some reason for you to be at X.

[8] See the references there to III 1, p. 601, and to III 13, p. 825.

[9] A similar point is made about passions at II 6, p. 271: "Now these passions which touch only the rind of us cannot be called ours. To make them ours, the whole man must be involved."

[10] This conclusion seems to be contradicted by statements like "No reward falls due to a virtue, however great, that has passed into a custom" (II 7, p. 276), or by Montaigne's repeated insistence that virtue presupposes difficulty and contrast (see,

In a well-purified soul such as [Socrates'], prepared by a continual exercise of wisdom and virtue, it is likely that these inclinations [that came to him without awaiting the advice of his reason], although instinctive and undigested, were always important and worth following. Everyone feels within himself some likeness of such stirrings of a prompt, vehement, and accidental opinion. It is my business to give them some authority, since I give so little to our wisdom. (I 11, pp. 29–30)

Thus one's virtue is what one *is*, and one's virtue is to be identified not with virtuous actions performed now and then, but with a consistent behavioral pattern, such as long, patient training can impose on one. "That is why," incidentally, "to judge a man, we must follow his traces long and carefully" (II 1, p. 243). In conclusion, Montaigne agrees with the view suggested above that practical knowledge—the knowledge of practices that have become well-entrenched reactions to the environment—is knowledge of (part of) the subject, and we are justified in seeing in his statement that "all he knows is himself" not so much the recognition of an annoying defect as a provocative suggestion of an important reversal in the conception of what it is to know, or to remember. The knowledge and the memory that matter—those that really have an impact on the world and on our own lives—are the automatic, unreflective, often unconscious knowledge of how to do things, the memory that is impressed not so much in our minds as in our moves: they are the knowledge and memory of what makes us ourselves. The other kind—the kind Montaigne does *not* have—is not worth having.

[E]ach man, instead of incorporating [truth and its precepts] into his behavior, incorporates them into his memory, very stupidly and uselessly. (I 23, p. 83)

To know by heart is not to know; it is to retain what we have given our memory to keep. What we know rightly we dispose

---

for example, II 11, p. 307). I will return to such contradictions later, in the context of an analysis of the important tensions Montaigne's position must face.

of, without looking at the model, without turning our eyes toward our book. (I 26, p. 112)

The Whole Man

It is Montaigne's conviction that a human being is no more soul than he is body, or vice versa. "Aristippus," he says, "defended the body alone, as if we had no soul; Zeno embraced only the soul, as if we had no body. Both were wrong" (III 13, p. 850). Education must take this interrelation into account, and insist on running and wrestling as much as on philosophy and the sciences, since "[i]t is not a soul that is being trained, not a body, but a man, [and] these parts must not be separated" (I 26, p. 122). At times, his characterizations of the interrelation remind us of the one postulated by Kant between sensibility and understanding: it is not just that man can know because he has both, but every single cognitive act involves the participation of both. "May we not say that there is nothing in us during this earthly imprisonment that is purely either corporeal or spiritual . . . ?" (III 5, p. 681).[11]

One may read these passages as expressing a tendency toward materialism; after all, Montaigne has already denounced the impotence of mental contents, and there is no lack in him of statements

---

[11] There occur in the *Essays* many additional statements of the tight connection between body and soul (French *ame*, virtually interchangeable here with *esprit*, translated by Frame as *mind* and occasionally as *spirit* [or, for that matter, even as *soul*, for example at III 5, p. 641]—a passage [among many] supporting the stated interchangeability can be found in the context of the quote below from III 12, p. 809, where *ame* and *esprit* occur only three lines apart from one another, and clearly in the same sense [*Oeuvres complètes*, p. 1035]). Body and soul (or mind) are judged to be our "two principal essential parts" (II 12, p. 386; see also footnote 6 of Chapter 6) and to have "a tight brotherly bond" (III 5, p. 641). We are told that "[t]here is nothing more likely than the conformity and relation of the body to the spirit" (III 12, p. 809), and even that "[m]y thoughts fall asleep if I make them sit down. My mind will not budge unless my legs move it" (III 3, p. 629). Thus the soul is urged "not to draw aside and entertain itself apart, not to scorn and abandon the body (nor can it do so except by some counterfeit monkey trick), but to rally to the body, embrace it, cherish it, assist it, control it, advise it, set it right and bring it back when it goes astray; in short, to marry it and be a husband to it" (II 17, pp. 484–85).

like "[t]he body has a great part in our being" (II 17, p. 484) or "it is a wonder how physical [man's] nature is" (III 8, p. 710). This tendency would only be natural in a man who is himself "wholly material, whom only reality satisfies, and a very massive reality" (III 9, p. 764), and who repeats over and over again that health—physical health—"should be our chief consideration" (I 39, p. 181) because it is "the finest and richest present that nature can give us" (II 12, p. 357), "worth purchasing by all the most painful cauteries and incisions that can be made" (II 37, p. 580).[12]

But no: if materialism is to have any bite, that is, if it is intended to reduce the significance or importance of the soul to that of the body, then it is entirely out of place here. Montaigne is quite the opposite of a reductionist, of any kind, and he is not blind to the mystery of how human components of such a vastly different nature *can* interrelate with each other, or of "how a spiritual impression can cut such a swath in a massive and solid object" (II 12, p. 402).[13] In fact, we will see that an interesting suggestion as to the resolution of this mystery is at least implicit in his work—one that has nothing whatsoever to do with reductionism. So if he emphasizes the importance of the body, it is largely to counter the traditional tendency of intellectuals to devalue it. His point is but a specific application of the general attitude I already attributed to him: no component of a man must be forgotten when one is searching for oneself—quite the contrary, "each particle, each occupation, of a man betrays him and reveals him just as well as any other" (I 50, p. 220). Therefore, since parts of the body, especially the less "noble" ones, are the most likely components to fall by the wayside, he chooses to *focus* on them: on the penis, of which he says that "no other [part] makes [him] more properly a man than this one" (III 5, p. 677), or on the kidney stones, whose cure suggests to him the reflection that "nothing is engendered in a body except by the connivance and commu-

---

[12] See also II 17, p. 487; III 12, p. 810.
[13] One of the sentences inscribed by Montaigne on his library reads (approximately: the sentence is very damaged, and what follows is a conjectural reconstruction): "Since you ignore how the soul is joined to the body, you do not know the work of God" (adapted from *Ecclesiastes; Oeuvres complètes*, p. 1421).

nication of all the parts. The whole mass works together, although one part contributes more than the other according to the diversity of operations" (II 37, p. 592).

We saw earlier that Montaigne's attitude is antiphilosophical, in that he does not want to separate and abstract but rather to spread and assimilate. We are now in a position to see that not only philosophy is his polemical target, but intellectualism in general. For the intellectual, mastering the world means making it objective and hence, specifically, *distinguishing* in it a number of objects and distinguishing each of them from himself. The intellectual's aim is that of knowing *about* the world while he remains himself and does not get confused with the object of his knowledge. Montaigne's ideal, on the other hand, is that of a being who becomes one and the same with what he knows, who may not be able to trace precise lines of demarcation between himself and his object but nonetheless gives the best evidence of his knowledge by functioning effectively.

At times, his statements of this ideal sound too extreme, for example when he says: "A learned man is not learned in all matters; but the capable man is capable in all matters, even in ignorance" (III 2, p. 611). He does not mean, however, that the "capable" man is a sort of *Uebermensch* who dominates, and perhaps profits from, even his defects, but that this man is well adjusted to his environment, adapted to it—he knows as much as he has to, and beyond that does not carry unnecessary, heavy burdens:

> The least contemptible class of people seems to me to be those who, through their simplicity, occupy the lowest rank. . . . The morals and the talk of peasants I find commonly more obedient to the prescriptions of true philosophy than are those of our philosophers. The common people are wiser, because they are as wise as they need be. (II 17, p. 501; last sentence quoted from Lactantius)

Life is easy and pleasant for those who rely on this practical, unconscious wisdom, "a wisdom not so ingenious, robust, and pompous as that of [the philosophers'] invention, but correspondingly easy and salutary, performing very well what the other talks about"

(III 13, p. 822). And apparently this is what Montaigne asks for himself: after all, he who says of himself that he is the matter of his book also says that he likes "only pleasant and easy books" (I 39, p. 181). What this means, in view of the above, is that he aspires to that syntony of moves, to that harmonious agreement of propensities and reactions, to that consistency, which more than anything make a man one, since they make it possible for him to function as one. Even his obsessive concern with health[14] should be seen in this light, since health is nothing but "maintaining [one's] accustomed state without disturbance" (III 13, p. 827), that is, manifesting the resilience that is typical of a *coherent* structure, a structure that follows its own laws of preservation and growth, and does not go the way the wind blows. Minds, on the other hand, or their most specific faculties—understanding and reason—if left to themselves and not kept "busy with some definite subject that will bridle and control them" (I 8, p. 21), are "unruly," "vague," "supple," and "erratic."[15] Which is why intellectuals, who turn the use of their minds into a profession, end up confusing instead of instructing, and "those who reconcile jurists with each other should first reconcile each one with himself" (II 12, p. 377).

We will see later that this peroration in favor of the ordinary, simple, "whole" man is not to be taken at face value, and that Montaigne in fact sides more with the unruly components of his bewildering self than he usually cares to admit. But before complicating matters even further, it is worth investigating how man is supposed to *become* whole.

Custom Rules

Two complementary instructions will lead us to the realization, in ourselves or others, of Montaigne's integrated human being: one negative and one positive. The negative one consists of making ourselves insensitive to the noisy questioning of reason, of regressing

---

[14] The best document of this obsession is certainly the *Travel Journal*.
[15] For these terms, see I 4, p. 15; III 11, p. 785; ibid., p. 792.

into a purely animal state: "Do you want a man to be healthy, do you want him disciplined and firmly and securely poised? Wrap him in darkness, idleness, and dullness. We must become like the animals in order to become wise, and be blinded in order to be guided" (ibid., p. 363).

The mind insists on having intellectual control on action, on deliberating on things before doing them, and on convincing itself (and its carrier) that things are done a certain way *because of* the results of deliberation. In fact, however, even "those who conduct [the most glorious exploits of war] make use of deliberation and counsel only for form. . . . There occur amid their deliberations fortuitous rejoicings and extraneous frenzies" (I 24, p. 93). Which is just as well, since "all that our wisdom can do is not much" (ibid.), and hence the best course is to forget it.

We have already encountered the second, positive instruction: it is repetition. "I wish Paluel or Pompey," Montaigne says, "those fine dancers of my time, could teach us capers just by performing them before us and without moving us from our seats" (I 26, p. 112), but this is not going to happen. To acquire the technical mastery of one's movements that makes them look natural, or even easy, there is only one recipe: continuous, patient, painstaking practice. And not just practice in general, not just familiarity with the whole enterprise of dancing, with its aims, strategies, or rewards, but practice of detail: "It is not enough to toughen [one's] soul; we must also toughen his muscles" (ibid., p. 113). Each muscle must be toughened, so that it will not give way at the wrong time; each movement must be tried out until it is (second) nature. Then, and only then, dancing becomes us, and we become dancers: "By long usage this form of mine has turned into substance, and fortune into nature" (III 10, p. 773).[16]

---

[16] For a more explicit articulation of this use of the word "nature" consider the following passage: "If what Nature flatly and originally demands of us for the preservation of our being is too little . . . then let us grant ourselves something further: let us also call the habits and condition of each of us *nature*. . . . Habit is a second nature, and no less powerful" (ibid., p. 772). I will return to the ambiguity of words like "nature" and "natural" at the beginning of Chapter 5.

As I suggested, these two instructions are not unconnected, and there is probably no way that application of one can be completed before turning to the other. The blind and single-minded dedication that dancing practice requires would be impossible if the pupil kept thinking of how many other things he could be doing instead, and of whether perhaps he *wants* to do them. At the same time, however, practicing dance blindly and single-mindedly is a very effective tactic for voiding one's mind of questions and worries, or, if you will, for voiding oneself of a (questioning and worrying) mind. The best way to think of the process may be as an analogue of a double recursion: a little forgetfulness makes it possible to concentrate on practicing for awhile, then the practicing brings with it more forgetfulness, and so on.

There are two (again, not unconnected) aspects to this primacy of practice and training. First, the primacy is a matter of *fact*: "[C]ustom and length of time are far stronger counselors than any other compulsion" (I 14, p. 36). Whether it is conducted from the outside or from the inside (through the will), any attempt at forcing us into some kind of behavior is going to remain largely ineffective unless it is sustained by that automatic concatenation of moves that only long familiarity with the moves may have taught us:

> Reasoning and education, though we are willing to put our trust in them, can hardly be powerful enough to lead us to action, unless besides we exercise and form our soul by experience to the way we want it to go; otherwise, when it comes to the time for action, it will undoubtedly find itself at a loss. (II 6, p. 267)

In fact, those who think that our inward affections influence (our will, which in turn influences) our external behavior are probably under a delusion. Quite often, what happens is the reverse; thus an orator "will imprint on himself a real and essential sorrow by means of this mummery that he enacts" (III 4, p. 636), and similarly one "could hardly be made to believe that the sight of our crucifixes . . . , the ornaments and ceremonious movements in our churches,

. . . do not warm the souls of the people with religious emotion very beneficial in effect" (II 12, p. 381).[17]

Second, the primacy of custom is also a matter of *duty*. Not only does custom rule: it *should* rule. Not only is habit "the most effective teacher of all things" (I 23, p. 77; quoted from Pliny): it is also, apparently, the most just. The conservative implications of this claim are obvious; nor, for that matter, does Montaigne leave them implicit. The way we are brought up is the way we should behave, he says: "[I]t is the rule of rules, and the universal law of laws, that each man should observe those of the place he is in" (ibid., p. 86). When somebody proposes a new policy, the burden is on him to demonstrate that his proposal is worth the trouble of bringing about the change: "[H]e must be very sure that he sees the weakness of what he is casting out and the goodness of what he is bringing in" (ibid., p. 88). As for himself, Montaigne says quite simply: "I am disgusted with innovation, in whatever guise" (ibid., p. 86).[18]

I said that these two aspects of the primacy of practice are related. The relation is of a complex nature, analogous to the double recursion mentioned above. To begin with, habit confers authority. When the mind and its inquiring attitude have been put to sleep by

---

[17] At times, Montaigne goes even further, to suggest a "behavioristic" account of emotions. He suggests, for example, that being enraged is simply looking enraged (see II 31, pp. 541–42).

[18] Later in the book, I will often use the word "revolution" and its cognates in contexts such as this, to bring out more clearly the relevance of Montaigne's view to contemporary concerns. Thus it may be useful to insist here that, in the essay from which this quote is taken, Montaigne mobilizes all essential traits of a revolution. There is change ("*changement*"—*Oeuvres complètes*, p. 118) and specifically political change ("*mutations d'estat*"—ibid., p. 119), change of an accepted law ("*changement d'une loy receue*"—ibid., p. 118); there is innovation ("*nouvelleté*"—ibid.), ambition ("*affectation ambitieuse*"—ibid. p. 117), usurpation of authority ("*L'autre . . . usurpe l'authorité de juger*"—ibid., p. 120), violence ("*violence*"—ibid., p. 121); there is precipitation ("*La majesté royalle . . . s'avale plus difficilement du sommet au milieu qu'elle ne se precipite du milieu à fons*"—ibid., p. 118), dislocation and dissolution ("*ce grand bastiment ayant esté desmis et dissout*"—ibid.), and risk ("*Mais le meilleur pretexte de nouvelleté est très-dangereux*"—ibid., p. 119). All these traits were familiar to Montaigne from the religious and political troubles of his times. But whatever the historical source of their impact on him, he has interesting things to say about them, and about why they should be confined to a theoretical plan; later we will explore the details.

long familiarity, certain forms of behavior begin to look not only natural but necessary, unshakable, unquestionable: "[N]o laws are held in their true honor except those to which God has given some ancient duration, so that no one knows their origin or that they were ever different" (I 43, p. 198).[19] An obvious consequence of the respect so acquired by ancient customs is that breaking them becomes inevitably associated with guilt, and at this point the step from facts to values is already made: "Each man, holding in inward veneration the opinions and the behavior approved and accepted around him, cannot break loose from them without remorse, or apply himself to them without self-satisfaction" (I 23, p. 83). But, in turn, this guilt makes it even more difficult to go against tradition and even more natural to go along with it. For guilt weakens man and innocence strengthens him. Speaking of torture, Montaigne says: "[T]he guilty man's conscience seems to abet the torture in making him confess his fault, and to weaken him; whereas the innocent man's conscience seems to fortify him against his torture" (II 5, p. 266). Thus, once again, the circle is closed: because of the hold it has on people, the behavior sanctioned by tradition is also regarded as good, and because it is regarded as good its hold becomes even stronger.

Some will say that the above cannot be the whole story: that it is not enough to say *that* custom is conducive to authority but one must also inquire whether this association *should* hold, and that thinking otherwise commits one to a kind of naturalistic fallacy. And so it may well be. The relevant point here is that the above is not even the whole of *Montaigne's* story. He has interesting things to add about the guilt of breaking rules, and though such things may not satisfy those who worry about naturalism, they do provide a useful articulation of his position. But the time for this articulation has not yet come.

[19] See also III 12, pp. 324–25; ibid., p. 403; III 13, p. 821. With lesser things, habit can establish authority much more quickly: "When [our people] wore the busk of their doublet between their breasts, they maintained with heated arguments that it was in its proper place; some years after, it has slipped down between the thighs, and they laugh at their former custom and find it absurd and intolerable" (I 49, p. 216).

CHAPTER THREE

THE TROUBLE WITH HABIT

Besides, perhaps I have some personal obligation
to speak only by halves, to speak confusedly, to
speak discordantly.
(*III 9, p. 762*)

ॐ

Tensions beneath the Surface

THERE ARE WAYS in which the argument in Chapter 2 develops
consistently the suggestions offered in Chapter 1. The self is not a
ready-made entity, available for inspection and analysis. It must be
constituted before it can be inspected, and its constitution requires
long, painstaking discipline: it requires that we forget the delusion
of "always already" exercising (rational?) control over our actions
and begin to pay careful, humble attention to the details of our
moves, looking for a logic that is implicit in them, recording that
logic on paper, and then committing the subject to it—a subject that
comes into being precisely through this commitment. This operation is empirical in nature, and as such definitely a posteriori: it does
not manifest the certainty that is expected of planning ahead, and
the rigid barriers that such certainty demands. When the first caper
was tried by the first dancer, that person was not yet a dancer, and
that movement was not yet a caper: it was a spontaneous way of
releasing excess energy, of expressing joy, perhaps. But then one
caper succeeded another, and on the way they *became* capers, as people started focusing on them, identifying them, and using them deliberately to express or to *communicate* their joy. Now there may be

"experts" who tell us exactly how a caper must be done, what a perfect caper is; but to some extent we all know this is nonsense. Chance and improvisation will bring about "deviant" capers in the future, some of them will stick, and the practice of expressing joy will continue to develop—beyond any fences anybody might care to erect: "[T]hose who would combat usage with grammar make fools of themselves" (III 5, p. 667). Similarly, my self will continue to develop in ways I cannot predict now, unless of course my "prediction" is the mystifying trick of ruling out certain developments as not possibly being mine, the verbal sorcery of bringing the I's genie back into the bottle by calling "I" *whatever* is in the bottle.

But there are also ways in which this development dialectically counters those suggestions, makes them grow along paths that are unexpected and a little puzzling, and forces us to look at them again, to see if perhaps there isn't something there that we missed at first. For, to begin with, the emphasis in all the discussion on training was on the silent, unconscious wisdom that one expresses by making the right move at the right time—in clear, dramatic contrast to the foolish pride of those who consign their "knowledge" to books. But then why should Montaigne search for himself precisely by writing a book? Why should he, who has no (propositional) memory, look for a substitute of it, and say of himself: "For lack of a natural memory I make one of paper" (III 13, p. 837)? After all, doesn't he *also* say, consistently with the discussion above, that "[w]hatever [he] may be, [he] want[s] to be elsewhere than on paper" (II 37, p. 596)?

The answer to these questions articulated in the first chapter and briefly rehearsed here is: Montaigne needs his book to become some one definite object. Without his book, and without the commitment the book imposes, he would be nothing definite at all. But, in the light of the analysis carried out in Chapter 2, couldn't we simply conclude that it does not matter: that the definiteness sought here is precisely that delusional, bookish narrowing down of life that the truly wise should reject, while he remains open to the multifarious ways the practices will take, to the gradual, relentless spreading that will eventually contradict all definitions, all determinations of an essence? Who *needs* a commitment here? Who needs to say what the self will *have* to be (descriptively *or* self-prescriptively)?

And then, in uneasy coordination with this first worry, a second one arises, which makes things even more confused. The point of training—however chancy its origins and blind its process—is stability. We do things over and over again to imprint them on ourselves, to become able to duplicate them identically, without deliberation, without even thinking. And we imprint them on ourselves this way because they represent a successful adaptation to the environment, and so long as the environment does not change, it is most productive to stick to what has worked so far. Which makes one think that dancing may be the wrong example after all, insofar as dancing is something we (seem to) do for its own sake, whereas most things we (seem to) do for the sake of something else:[1] of surviving and prospering primarily, and then of a number of other, more specific, activities that are instrumental to those. When this pragmatic dimension is properly stressed, conservatism becomes a fundamental value, and training the most powerful tool one has to enforce it. Montaigne, we know, is aware of these implications, and comes down repeatedly, loud and clear, on the side of tradition. Not always, however: sometimes his statements are revisionary, or even radical, in nature. Thus, for example, ethnocentrism is for him a frequent polemical objective:

> [W]e should beware of clinging to vulgar opinions, and judge things by reason's way, not by popular say. (I 31, p. 150)

> We call contrary to nature what happens contrary to custom. . . . Let this universal and natural reason drive out of us the error and astonishment that novelty brings us. (II 30, p. 539)[2]

---

[1] But see the following passage: "And I walk for the sake of walking. Those who run after a benefice or a hare do not run; they only run who run at prisoner's base and to practice running" (III 9, p. 747). It suggests that an action is performed properly only when it is performed for its own sake. I will return later to this non (act) utilitarian view.

[2] See also I 5, p. 16; II 12, p. 330; ibid., p. 358; ibid., p. 391; III 8, p. 709.

And occasionally we find him saying that "natural inclination . . . must lead to frequent mistakes" (II 8, p. 291), or that "all those predispositions that are born in us without reason are bad; they are a kind of disease that we must combat" (II 37, p. 580). Not to mention passages like the following, which strike one as clear pronouncements in favor of the "unruly" and "erratic" component of our personality (or is it perhaps the other side, now, that is unruly and erratic?): "In that windy confusion of rumors, reports, and popular opinions that push us about, no worth-while road can be charted. Let us not set ourselves a goal so fluctuating and wavering: let us steadfastly follow reason" (II 16, p. 473).

And it is not just a matter of what he *says*. It is also, and more important, a matter of what he *does*, of his behavior and strategy. True, he held public office as mayor of Bordeaux, and his balance and conscientiousness during a troubled time of religious wars (well attested by his *Letters*)[3] brought him the signal honor of a reelection for a second term—an honor that, he recalls proudly, had been conferred "only twice before" (III 10, p. 768). But he describes this office as having been imposed on him, and himself as resisting it as far as feasible: "Messieurs of Bordeaux elected me mayor of their city when I was far from France and still farther from such a thought. I excused myself, but I was informed that I was wrong, since the king's command also figured in the matter" (ibid.).[4] He knows that participating in the public administration is something

[3] Twenty-three of the thirty-nine letters we have date from the period of Montaigne's mayoralty (1581–85) and are connected with the various duties of his office. As for the balance and conscientiousness they reveal, a couple of examples will do. In *Letter* 32, Montaigne writes to the Jurats of Bordeaux: "As for that bad example and the injustice of taking women and children prisoners, I do not at all think that we should imitate it as others have done. I have said this also to the said lord marshal" (p. 1089). In *Letter* 30, he writes to Matignon (the "said lord marshal" of the previous quote): "I have spent every night either around the town in arms or outside of town at the port, and before your warning I had already kept watch there one night on the news of a boat loaded with armed men which was due to pass" (p. 1087).

[4] Consider also the following note made by Montaigne on his copy of Beuther's *Éphémérides*: "1577, Henry of Bourbon king of Navarre without my knowledge and in my absence had sent to me in Leitoure a nomination as gentleman of his chamber" (*Oeuvres complètes*, p. 1408).

he "owe[s] the world out of civic duty" (III 3, p. 630), he has seen his father, who held the same post before him, "his soul cruelly agitated by this public turmoil, forgetting the sweet air of his home, . . . and his household and his health, . . . truly heedless of his life, which he nearly lost in this" (III 10, p. 769), but "[t]his course, which [he] commend[s] in others, [he does] not love to follow" (ibid.). In fact, it is an interesting, revealing coincidence that his first election as mayor came to interrupt an activity that he really enjoyed: that of traveling through foreign countries.

Others are urged not to leave their ordinary habitat: "You have quite enough to do at home; don't go away" (ibid., p. 767). And this advice is consistent with his remark, noted earlier, that one should address oneself with earnest dedication to the task of appreciating one's situation in life and "loyally responding to and satisfying every part of one's charge" (II 33, p. 555). But he does not like to follow his own advice: he likes to (and does) travel, and he uses his travels to counteract the *limitations* of habit. His *Travel Journal* contains a detailed record of how he indulged in this inclination for a period of seventeen months and eight days between 1580 and 1581, right after the publication of the first edition of the *Essays*, and of the pleasure he experienced in so indulging. According to the journal (partly compiled by a secretary), "the pleasure [Montaigne] took in visiting unknown countries, . . . he found so sweet as to make him forget the weakness of his age and of his health" (*Travel Journal*, p. 915).[5] He was forever interested in "*essay[ing]* completely the diversity of manners and customs" (ibid., p. 884; italics mine), to the point that he "wanted to see the rooms to let and the conditions of the boarding houses" in order "to try out [*essayer*] all the comforts of [Florence], as he had of [other cities]" (ibid., p. 932), that he "tried [*esséia*] covering himself in bed with a feather quilt, as is [the Germans'] custom" (ibid., p. 891), and regretted "that he had

[5] In fact, the journal gives the impression that Montaigne is healthier when traveling away from home than when returning home or staying at the baths. And, in contrast with other statements of his to be quoted later (see footnote 2 of Chapter 4 and the attending text), he says at ibid., p. 960, that "[t]here is nothing so hostile to [his] health as boredom and idleness."

not brought along a cook to instruct in [foreign] ways so that some-
day the cook could try them [*en . . . faire la preuve*] at home" (ibid.,
p. 892). He "strenuously avoided passing over the same road twice"
(ibid., p. 903),[6] and declared himself to feel especially at ease in
Rome because it is a city of "resident, domiciled foreigners" (ibid.,
p. 962).[7] With the result that "there entered into his judgment a bit
of passion, a certain scorn for his country, which he regarded with
hatred and indignation" (ibid., p. 892),[8] and in general, a distrust of
"other people's judgment on the matter of the conveniences of foreign countries, since every man's taste is governed by the ordering
of his habit and the usage of his village" (ibid., p. 910). Thus he
traveled "very fed up with [the French] ways" (III 9, p. 754)[9] and
considered it "a great disadvantage" when abroad to be with people
of one's own country, "inasmuch as this society accustoms [one] to
the ways and language of [his] own nation and deprives [him] of the
means of acquiring foreign acquaintances" (*Travel Journal*, p. 919).

Nor does his restlessness stop when he does not travel. The other
activity he enjoys most and to which he dedicates most of his time
and energy—his reading and writing ("In my library I spend most
of the days of my life, and most of the hours of the day," he says at
III 3, p. 629)—is just as destabilizing as travel is, or more.[10] "If to

---

[6] See also p. 906, where Montaigne makes a trip just to see a place; p. 935, where
he regrets that his mule draws him away from a sight; and p. 1014, where the scene
"continually changing" gives him enough "matter to feed [his] curiosity."

[7] At ibid., p. 961, Rome is called "the most universal city in the world" and one
where "everyone is as if at home" (see a similar remark about philosophy on p. 78
below), and at III 9, p. 763, "the only common and universal city."

[8] See also ibid., p. 947.

[9] See also I 26, p. 106, "a little of everything and nothing thoroughly, French
style." But in *Letter* 9, p. 1065 (where what is in question is not his private games,
but real life), he writes: "You and me, my wife, let us live in the old French way."

[10] At times, Montaigne points to a strong analogy between traveling and reading.
Thus in *Travel Journal*, p. 915, he is reported as saying "that he seemed to be rather
like people who are reading some very pleasing story and therefore begin to be afraid
that soon it will come to an end, or any fine book; so he took such pleasure in traveling that he hated to be nearing each place where he was to rest, and toyed with
several plans for traveling as he pleased, if he could get away alone." And at III 3, p.
628 we are told that he never "travel[s] without books, either in peace or in war," but
that "many days will pass, and even some months, without [his] using them." The

philosophize is to doubt," he says, "then to play the fool and follow
my fancies, as I do, is all the more to doubt" (II 3, p. 251). Once
again, what he does is to test, and testing is precisely what brings
about that doubt which is so destructive of our trust in ancient institutions: "The reason why we doubt hardly anything is that we
never test [*essaye*] our common impressions. We do not probe the
base, where the fault and weakness lies; we dispute only about the
branches" (II 12, p. 403).

So Montaigne's behavior is directly counter to most of his rec-
ommendations: if others are best advised to put their reason to sleep
because, as Plato thinks, "there is some sinful impiety in inquiring
too curiously into God and the world, and the first causes of things"
(ibid., p. 369), he keeps *his* reason well awake, and lends his ear
ruthlessly to the most sinful curiosity. If to others he recommends
moderation and respect of tradition, he himself "seek[s] out change
indiscriminately and tumultuously" (III 9, p. 761).[11] Why? Is he perhaps convinced, like Plato, that knowledge is not for everybody,
and that "several opinions [possibly including the opinion one is to
reach about oneself by an investigation such as his] . . . are better
hushed up than published to weak minds" (II 12, p. 439)? Perhaps,
but this is not enough of an answer.

Beware of Darkness

Habit is subject to at least two specific criticisms, according to
Montaigne. First, it is a source of inhibition: "Wherever I want to
turn, I have to force some barrier of custom, so carefully has it
blocked all our approaches" (I 36, p. 166). We do things because

interesting reason is that there is continuity between reading and "any other kind of
amusement," and he would "sooner accept [the latter], however, trivial, because
[reading] cannot fail [him]."

[11] The context of this quote adds an important qualification, since it makes it clear
that the change Montaigne seeks out so passionately is in the area of literary style
(whereas when it comes to "real" action, as we have seen, he is quite moderate and
conservative). Later in the book I will address the issue of why his revolutionary
pronouncements should be confined to language.

they have always been done that way, and we have long forgotten why. Our reaction to alternatives borders on psychopathology: it expresses itself in irrational, unmotivated denial, and sometimes in plain horror.

> Darius asked certain Greeks for how much they would adopt the Indian custom of eating their dead fathers . . . ; they answered him that not for anything in the world would they do it. And when he tried to persuade the Indians to give up their practice and adopt that of Greece, which was to burn their fathers' bodies, he horrified them still more. (I 23, p. 84)[12]

Of course, everyone has stories that rationalize one's habits; the Indians, for example, thought "that they could not give . . . a more favorable sepulture than in themselves" (ibid.). But how much are we to believe these stories, when we consider that the opinions "are apt to be [most commonly followed] which most suit our inclinations" (II 16, p. 470), and that "good minds have [great facility] of making whatever they like seem true" (II 12, p. 429)?[13] Inevitably, the suspicion insinuates itself that usage, by imposing its power on us and depriving us of the view of all options, "robs us of the true appearance of things" (I 23, p. 84).

Two remarks are in order here, concerning this negative judgment passed on habit. First, note how the judgment results not from a change in what Montaigne believes, but from a curious reversal of values. The same fact that was formerly cited in favor of traditional behavior and training—that is, the fact that they become second nature, set up a system of automatic responses, and thus by-

---

[12] At II 2, p. 250, Montaigne says that "[a]ll actions outside the ordinary limits are subject to sinister interpretation," and at I 31, p. 158, speaking of "the cannibals," that "[t]ruly here are real savages by our standards; for either they must be thoroughly so, or we must be."

[13] See also I 23, p. 79 ("I think that there falls into man's imagination no fantasy so wild that it does not match the example of some public practice, and for which, *consequently*, our reason does not find a stay and a foundation" [italics mine]); II 12, p. 438 ("See how reason provides plausibility to different actions. It is a two-handled pot, that can be grasped by the left or the right"); II 17, p. 496 ("in whatever direction I turn, I can always provide myself with enough causes and probabilities to keep me that way").

pass meddlesome reason's control (and worries)—is now regarded as a crucial defect. It is as if two different people were looking at the same thing and not disagreeing on *what* the thing is but on whether they *like* it; we will see later that this strange, almost schizophrenic mixture of personalities (and of values) is a crucial aspect of Montaigne's perplexing strategy.

Second, note that the same reversal of values applies to the other major dialectical element at work here. The "unruliness" of mind is now seen as a truly liberating factor, which will help us break the strictures imposed by blind custom. "[I]t is always a vice to enslave yourself," Montaigne says (III 13, pp. 843–44), and that of tradition is true slavery, from which independent judgment will release us:

> And where others are swept—either by the custom of their country, or by their parental upbringing, or by chance—as by a tempest, without judgment or choice, indeed most often before the age of discretion, to such or such an opinion, . . . to which they find themselves pledged, enslaved, and fastened as to a prey they have bitten into and cannot shake loose . . . why shall it not be granted similarly to these men to maintain their liberty, and to consider things without obligation and servitude? (II 12, p. 373)

The second criticism Montaigne addresses to habit is that it makes one weaker: he himself, we are told, owes "many . . . weaknesses to habit" (III 13, p. 831). If we look at the reason for this criticism, once again we face the reversal of values that was mentioned above. Habit is the best way to integrate oneself in a given environment: through it we become part of that environment, and the moves that are best adapted to it come "natural," and even easy, to us. But what from one point of view is a maximum of effectiveness, from another is a minimum of flexibility, and Montaigne seems to take more pride[14] in the latter quality than in the former:

---

[14] This is only rational, given the significance that pride will gradually acquire in our discourse. For a first statement to this effect, see p. 46 below.

The best of my bodily qualities is that I am flexible and not very stubborn. . . . A young man should violate his own rules to arouse his vigor and keep it from growing moldy and lax. And there is no way of life so stupid and feeble as that which is conducted by rules and discipline. (Ibid., p. 830)[15]

While the body is still supple, it should for that reason be bent to all fashions and customs. And provided his appetite and will can be kept in check, let a young man boldly be made fit for all nations and companies, even for dissoluteness and excess, if need be. (I 26, p. 123)

Thus, whereas elsewhere he incites us to become like the animals and put our reason to sleep, in a number of passages he reacts quite strongly against the blindness derived from unreflectiveness, the darkness into which a single-minded attitude precipitates us, and the stupidity that affects all resulting behavior. At times, he seems completely to reverse himself and claims that the stories our mind tells to rationalize our behavior—empty and delusive as they may be—confer some dignity to what would otherwise be "merely a stupid and thoughtless inclination" (II 37, p. 597).

Ordinarily, however, his judgments cut two ways. When he says that "wisdom forbids you to be satisfied with yourself and trust yourself, and always sends you away discontented and diffident, whereas opinionativeness and heedlessness fill their hosts with rejoicing and assurance" (III 8, p. 716),[16] one might read this as a praise of folly if confidence and certainty are taken as fundamental values, or conversely as a way of letting certainty down, if you don't want to be a fool.[17] Analogous remarks apply when he reminds us

[15] The context of this passage is interestingly complex, since it makes it clear that Montaigne regards this flexibility, too, as a result of habit, indeed as "the noblest and most useful of its teachings." (Similar remarks apply to the next quote.) I will return to this issue at the very end of the present chapter, and then again in Chapter 5.

[16] At I 26, p. 111, he says more concisely: "Only the fools are certain and assured."

[17] This conflict of values is perhaps best expressed by the paradoxical statement at II 12, p. 404: "The impression of certainty is a certain token of folly and extreme uncertainty."

that "[e]rror and dreams serve [the soul] usefully, being suitable stuff for giving us security and contentment" (I 14, p. 39). Finally, when he agrees with "our masters" that "[a] man must be a little mad if he does not want to be even more stupid" (III 9, p. 761), you have your choice of evils: would you rather be brutish or crazy? Those who like it simple might complain that he seems to put his eggs in no basket at all; but Montaigne, in spite of what he says,[18] does not like it simple, and his statements to the contrary are one more complication we will have to face in due time.

The Seven-Year Itch

The situation we face is one of bewildering confusion. While expressing the most conservative views, Montaigne proceeds in fact as a revolutionary, insinuating in the minds of his readers dangerous doubts on the foundations of what is considered acceptable behavior, and occasionally his statements go along with this restlessness and become subtle (or not so subtle; see the necrophagy mentioned earlier) exhortations to rebellion. While teaching us the power of habit, and what "a very favorable gift of nature" habit is "for a wretched condition such as ours" in that it "benumbs our senses to the suffering of many ills" (III 9, p. 741), he prefers his senses to be working, claims "not [to be] content" with "[a] somber, dull tranquillity . . . [that] puts [him] to sleep and stupefies [him]" (III 5, p. 640), considers "[r]epetition . . . boring anywhere," and "dislike[s] inculcation, even of useful things" (III 9, p. 734).[19] While telling us that consistency is the most important value to strive for, that it is what ultimately makes one *one*, and *this* one rather than another, and warning us that such consistency is a hard-won prize, to be awarded only after a long investigation of the minute details of one's most recondite moves, he comes out in the open claiming that "we are wrong to try to compose a continuous body out of all this suc-

[18] See I 26, p. 127: "The speech I love is a simple, natural speech."
[19] Once again, it is *verbal* repetition and inculcation that he claims to dislike in this passage. See footnote 11 above.

cession of feelings" (I 38, p. 174), that "even good authors are wrong to insist on fashioning a consistent and solid fabric out of us" (II 1, p. 239), and that he wishes "fewer people would meddle" with the "arduous and hazardous undertaking" of "prob[ing] the inside and discover[ing] what springs set men in motion" (ibid., p. 244). And while preaching that "[t]o compose our character is our duty, not to compose books" (III 13, p. 850), he does precisely the latter, and perhaps for this reason is eventually forced to admit that "there is nothing [he treats] specifically except nothing, and no knowledge except that of the lack of knowledge" (III 12, p. 809).

As with the emphasis on the physical nature of our being, which we discussed earlier, there may be a psychological basis for this perverse (?) inclination in favor of what seems to be useless and counterproductive—a basis not specific to the individual Montaigne but common to all of mankind. Though effective and economical, habit is also boring, and this feature may have a crucial role in making people desire novelty for novelty's sake. "Everything, no matter what it is, that falls within our knowledge and enjoyment, we find unsatisfactory" (I 53, p. 225).[20] "Do we think that choirboys take great pleasure in music? Not so; satiety makes it boring to them" (I 42, p. 193). The same goes for the goods available in a given place: the foreigners travel a long way to attain them, and the locals despise them. "It happens here as elsewhere," Montaigne says of the waters at La Villa, "that what we seek with so much difficulty is held in contempt by the people of the country" (*Travel Journal*, p. 998). And the same goes for physical beauty, for on the one hand "[e]very strange woman seems to us an attractive woman" (III 9, p. 745), and on the other "acquaintance and familiarity disgust us with one another" (II 12, p. 357)—so much so indeed that those (women) who know about it, and are artful and prudent enough, will be quite circumspect in admitting others to their presence, and cover more of themselves than they reveal. Even such an airy thing as words must fight a losing battle with this constitutional restlessness of human nature:

[20] See also I 54, p. 226; II 12, p. 342; II 15, p. 464; II 37, pp. 585–86; III 9, p. 723.

Of some of those words that I have just picked out it is harder
for us to perceive the energy, because the frequent use of them
has somewhat debased and vulgarized their grace for us; as in
our vernacular we encounter excellent phrases and metaphors
whose beauty is withering with age and whose color has been
tarnished by too common handling. (III 5, p. 666)[21]

So shall we conclude that Montaigne's is the rebelliousness of a
somewhat spoiled character, the starts of a proud thoroughbred
that, while recognizing the use of the saddle, still cannot bring itself
whole-heartedly to accept its burden? Maybe, but then again,
maybe not. At least there is a chance that the story is a little longer
and more interesting; after all, its author says that "there is nothing
useless in nature, not even uselessness itself" (III 1, p. 599), and
hence even that pride which is man's "ruin and his corruption . . .
[the] pride that casts man aside from the common ways, that makes
him embrace novelties and prefer to be the leader of an erring troop
. . . rather than to be . . . led and guided by another's hand, on the
straight and beaten path" (II 12, p. 368),[22] that pride which is especially useless and mad in a man who says he aspires to "order, consistency, and tranquillity of opinions and conduct" (II 17, p. 499),
must have a use after all.

One of my major goals in the rest of this book will be to explore
the pragmatic significance, if any, of the "useless" drive to change
and displacement, and such an exploration will require a long, con-
voluted detour (to begin in the next chapter) through those features
of Montaigne's, and of our, personality that are responsible for, and
active in, making him, and us, rebellious and proud. To bring the

---

[21] See II 36, p. 570, where Homer is reported as being "in Plutarch's judgment
. . . the only author in the world who has never sated or palled on men, appearing
ever entirely different to his readers, and ever blooming in new grace." Bad news (!)
for all other manipulators of words!

[22] See also III 7, p. 699 ("ambition never follows its own bent better than by some
out-of-the-way and unused path"), as well as two of the sentences inscribed on Montaigne's library: "The one who happens to consider himself a great man will be completely knocked down by the first pretext," and "The opinion that you have of your
importance will lose you, because you believe that you are somebody" (*Oeuvres complètes*, pp. 1420, 1424).

present chapter to a close, however, I find it helpful to emphasize a point of connection between the satisfaction of this drive and the features of habit and training discussed earlier. The point is this: just as it is not enough to *want* to do capers, or to *be told* how to do capers, for us to become able to do them, it is not enough for us to want to shake the tyranny of habit, or to be told that we could, or that we must. Precisely because habit is the result of long training, and because this training has made our muscles—not just our minds—learn its ways, we need an analogous training to *break away* from habit. The outcome of discipline can be erased only by more discipline, going in the opposite direction. If appropriating a technique takes work, disappropriating one that we have already gotten hold of—or, perhaps better, that has already gotten hold of us— takes as much, or more, work. This lesson, which Descartes tries to teach in the *Meditations*, is already implicit in the *Essays*.[23] Doubting is not only a choice: it is primarily a methodology, a perseverating strategy that step after step detaches us from our prejudices, trains us to face their "optional" character, and makes us strong enough to confront, for a moment at least, the void left by their fall, the nothingness on which they rely. The next moment, more likely than not, our dependence will surface again, as did Montaigne's when he desperately tried to mix with the natives during his travels.

> At last he had fallen into the fault that he most avoided, that of making himself noticeable by some mannerism at variance with the taste of those who saw him; for as far as in him lies, he conforms and falls into line with the ways of the place where he happens to be, and in Augsburg he wore a fur cap around the town. (*Travel Journal*, p. 900)[24]

[23] Consistently with this lesson, Montaigne suggests at times that even recreation and enjoyment require management and discipline. See III 3, pp. 629–30; III 13, p. 853. See also the next footnote.

[24] On the other hand, there are times when Montaigne seems to effectively counteract (and partially overcome) the limitations of habit by becoming familiar with a new environment. Thus, on November 22–24, 1580, he goes through Florence a first time, sees a few sights, visits some of the local dignitaries, but sounds uncomfortable and unappreciative, and remarks: "I do not know why this city should be privileged

Thus, once again, one need not forget any of the "facts" Montaigne has uncovered—in this case, about the peculiarities of habit—in order to appreciate the new, revolutionary point of view that he surprisingly throws at us. One need only adopt different values, and see those peculiarities as belonging to an enemy: an enemy that we can combat effectively, and possibly defeat, only if we match its sources of strength, and respond to its weapons, with something analogous in kind, not if we face its firepower with delusional wishful thinking. As for these different values, and how they can—perhaps uneasily, but still unfailingly—coexist with their opposites in one and the same person, we need to know more "facts" before we can attempt an explanation.

---

to be surnamed 'the beautiful' " (ibid., p. 930). Then, on June 22–July 2, 1581, he stays in Florence a third time (and for the longest time), and "finally confess[es] that Florence is rightly called 'the beautiful' " (ibid., p. 1006). And again, he says of Rome that "[t]he pleasures of residence in this city increased by more than half with acquaintance" (ibid., p. 965).

CHAPTER FOUR

MIND GAMES

It is a monstrous thing that I will say, but I will say it
all the same: I find . . . my lust less depraved than
my reason.

(*II 11, p. 312*)

᠅

The Razor's Edge

IN OUR SEARCH for Montaigne's view of the self, one component
of human nature has gradually come to occupy center stage. This
component, usually referred to as "mind" or "reason," is to be handled with extreme care. "The mind is a dangerous blade," Montaigne says, "even to its possessor, for anyone who does not know
how to wield it with order and discretion" (II 12, p. 420),[1] so
"[p]eople are right to give the tightest possible barriers to the human mind" (ibid., p. 419), to give it "blinkers to hold its gaze, in
subjection and constraint, in front of its feet" (ibid., p. 420). Setting
such limits "is not easy" (ibid., p. 421), and Montaigne himself—
we know already—is not of one mind (!) on this matter: at times he
welcomes the blinkers, and reminds us that "it is no good to be so

---

[1] See also ibid., p. 419 ("Our mind is an erratic, dangerous, and heedless tool"); II
17, p. 496 ("Human reason is a two-edged and dangerous sword"); and III 5, p. 670
("We are ingenious only in maltreating ourselves; that is the true quarry of the power
of our mind—a dangerous tool when out of control"). An interesting variant can be
found at II 12, p. 363, where mind is judged to be a danger for *itself*: "Countless
minds have been ruined by their very power and suppleness." At I 25, p. 103, this
risky character is predicated of learning, which is judged to be "a dangerous sword
that will hamper and hurt its master."

subtle and clever" (ibid., p. 419), and at other times does just the opposite, shakes all ties, and proclaims his "very favorite qualities" to be "idleness and freedom" (III 9, p. 741).[2] Now, however, such vague pronouncements no longer satisfy us: we know that, whatever is at stake in the constitution of a subject, it must involve the painful enterprise of challenge and rebellion, the proud calling in question of any establishment, the danger of inhibiting all conditioned reflexes and thereby losing all efficiency. So we need to know exactly *how* rebellion is needed to make a self, *why* there is tension between comfortable, reassuring tradition and the only too human business of thought, *what* the danger is of following one's call for freedom away from the beaten path. Answering these questions will take time and effort, as well as require us to address issues that are presently out of our sight; but it will all pay off in the end—or so we hope.

A natural start for our itinerary comes from the many passages where Montaigne says that mind, or reason, "does nothing but go astray in everything" (II 12, p. 386).[3] The point made here is one we are already familiar with: mind is unruly, it runs counter to custom, and tends to break down its prescriptions, confusing what seemed clear, shaking what seemed solid, dislocating what seemed unmovable. A useful qualification is added to this point when Montaigne uncovers a major characteristic of reason, and one that is central to its destabilizing activity: "[R]eason . . . is a supple tool, pliable, and adaptable to any form" (ibid., p. 403).[4] On the basis of this qualification, we begin to see how the process works. It is not that there is an agency in us whose explicit purpose is to contradict rules and reject principles of conduct—or at least we have no need to postulate the existence of such an agency. It is rather that no rule or principle will ever conquer and hold all of us: in spite of whatever training and conditioning we are subject to, there will (or perhaps may? or should?)[5] always remain a "soft core" of our being that is inaccessi-

---

[2] Or his "ruling qualities" to be "[f]reedom and laziness" (ibid., p. 759).

[3] See also ibid., p. 438; II 20, p. 511.

[4] See also I 23, p. 80; I 38, p. 173; II 12, p. 425; II 29, p. 537.

[5] Note the mixture of factual and evaluative terminology here, that is, ultimately,

ble to, and independent from, the training and the conditioning, and that is ready to take the most varied shapes, the most fantastic directions. "The body has, except for differences of degree, only one gait and one posture. The soul may be shaped into all varieties of forms, and molds to itself and to its every condition the feelings of the body and all other accidents" (I 14, p. 39).[6]

What is perhaps most perplexing about this soft core of our personality is the way it brings to the fore what is *not* the case. What is the case—obtuse, everyday reality—is best dealt with automatically and unreflectively, following the safe and assured lead of habit, so the mind would be at a loss competing with tradition and training on this ground. But the mind is interested in no such competition: its interest lies in unreality, its practice consists in concentrating on what does not happen. "There is no fancy so frivolous and so extravagant that it does not seem to me quite suitable to the production of the human mind" (III 8, p. 704).

Sometimes, this emphasis on the nonexistent takes the form of a concern with the future. Our reasons, Montaigne says, "often anticipate the fact, and extend their jurisdiction so infinitely that they exercise their judgment even in inanity and non-being" (III 11, p. 791).[7] This exercise is, of course, directly opposite in aim to the process of incorporation and assimilation of what is "ready-to-hand" that is most efficient and productive in dealing with the existent (in this case, present) state of affairs: "[A] notable example of the frenzied curiosity of our nature, which wastes its time anticipating future things, as if it did not have enough to do digesting the present" (I 11, p. 27).

---

of references to both efficient and final causes for the existence of such a "soft core." In the quasi-evolutionistic model to be drawn later, this mixture will find its justification. See note 22 of Chapter 5 and the attending text.

[6] To anticipate a point that will be made later, however, there is a suggestion here that the difference between soul and body is one of degree only. The same suggestion is made at II 32, p. 546: "[I]t is very hard to assign bounds to the achievements of the faculties of the soul, whereas we have more chance to assign limits to physical powers." And it is even clearer at II 37, p. 598: "[V]ariety is the most general fashion that nature has followed, and more in minds than bodies, inasmuch as minds are of a substance suppler and susceptible of more forms."

[7] See also I 3, p. 8.

But even limiting the mind to a temporal dimension is limiting it too much. The real object of the mind's interest, and the real playground for its games, is the *logical space*, by which I mean: the *space of possibilities*. In this connection, Montaigne says:

> Your reason is never more plausible and on more solid ground than when it convinces you of the plurality of worlds. (II 12, p. 390)

> Our reason is capable of filling out a hundred other worlds and finding their principles and contexture. It needs neither matter nor basis; let it run on; it builds as well on emptiness as on fullness, and with inanity as with matter.
> (III 11, p. 785)

Man is a counterfactual animal, not just a future-bent, goal-oriented one: his concern with what *will* be is but one aspect of his more general concern with what *can* be. "[H]e alone of all the animals has this freedom of imagination and this unruliness in thought that represents to him what is, what is not, what he wants, the false and the true" (II 12, p. 336). Psycho-logical purists may frown upon the apparent interchangeability of "imagination," "thought," "reason," and "mind" in contexts such as this one, and perhaps try to resolve the "ambiguities" of Montaigne's text by "sorting out" the tasks to be assigned to these different "faculties," but aside from such quibbles a number of points should be absolutely clear.

First, the mythopoetic activity of shaping alternative, fanciful world-stories is a dominating—indeed, characterizing—tendency of human beings: "And then how much it is to satisfy the imagination! In my opinion that faculty is all-important, at least more important than any other" (III 13, p. 833).[8]

Second, there is an obvious sense in which this activity opposes the entrenchment of *any* custom or rule. We know already that nothing is more indispensable for entrenchment than blind, single-minded dedication: without such dedication, the "double recursion" of training and habit will not even get started. And hence we know that nothing is more destructive for the prospects of that re-

---

[8] See also II 29, p. 537.

cursion than the "openness" generated by extending the range of options. This openness is distracting, and there is no worse enemy than distraction for those who want (or have) to concentrate. Even perceptual habits—those most immediately responsible for telling us what is the case—can be called in question by troublesome mind: "[I]t is marvelous how far the suppleness of our reason has followed [the Pyrrhonians] in this plan of combating the evidence of the facts" (II 12, p. 430).

Third, make no mistake on where Montaigne's preference lies in this dialectic. "There are authors whose end is to tell what has happened," he says, "[m]ine, if I could attain it, would be to talk about what *can* happen" (I 21, p. 75; italics mine). This is why he "most often" tries "some unaccustomed point of view" (I 50, p. 219). This is why "*[d]istinguo* is the most universal member of [his] logic" (II 1, p. 242): the *distinguo* that makes him say nothing about himself "absolutely, simply, and solidly, without confusion and without mixture, or in one word" (ibid.). And this is why "[t]he thing [he fears] most is fear" (I 18, p. 53): the fear that blocks us in front of the unknown, the fear that makes us look away from the strange, the new, the unfamiliar, the fear that prevents us from inventing and exploring. Poetry is free, he says, "and works as it will" (II 37, p. 576 footnote), and he also says of himself that he loves "the poetic gait, by leaps and gambols" (III 9, p. 761), and of what he does—that is, of philosophy—that it is "but sophisticated poetry" (II 12, p. 401).[9] In this fight for freedom at all costs and against all odds—for remember, he is "sick for freedom" (III 13, p. 820)—Montaigne lists even God on his side: the being that was, and is, for many but an excuse for imposition and tyranny becomes for him a "transcendental" (that is, a conceptual)[10] guarantee that there are no barriers to be found, at least not by us.

[R]eason has taught me that to condemn a thing thus, dogmatically, as false and impossible, is to assume the advantage of knowing the bounds and limits of God's will and of the

---

[9] See also ibid., p. 417; III 9, p. 761.

[10] For this identification between *transcendental* and *conceptual*, see my *Kant's Copernican Revolution*.

power of our mother Nature; and that there is no more notable folly in the world than to reduce these things to the measure of our capacity and competence. (I 27, p. 132)[11]

No matter how much *we* feel constrained by the "evidence" before
us, the Infinite Other will not be so constrained, and hence the
world will not be, either. The ultimate story is that there is no ultimate story, no *experimentum crucis*, no Archimedean fulcrum. Every
foundation can be shaken, and every certainty can be challenged:
for *this* claim, God will be my witness.

The Strategy of Imagination

I pointed out earlier that Montaigne's man is not a soul, or a body,
but an integrated structure of which those two are but different aspects: the result of adopting different (and equally limited) points of
view. But the last few wrinkles of my argument seem to go against
the spirit of that characterization, and suggest instead an uneasy association of two conflicting realities: a thick, opaque brute that
blindly reiterates, with an efficiency that is only matched by its lack
of imagination, moves that were made before, for no reason except
that they were made before,[12] and a confabulating, gratuitous
agency obsessively concerned with inventing stories about what
does not exist and does not matter, and stubbornly opposed to any
structure and any rest. Given how different the level is at which
these two realities operate, what is left of the alleged integration
suggested earlier? Do not these realities simply coexist (spatio-tem-
porally), without it being clear *how* and *why* they do? And since one
of them is often referred to as "mind," and the other clearly reso-
nates of a physical, animal kind of behavior, isn't the contrast be-

---

[11] See also II 12, p. 389. At ibid., p. 392, Montaigne says: "I do not think it is good
to confine the divine power thus under the laws of our speech." And at ibid., p. 393,
he suggests that God is not bound by our logic.

[12] Of course, there are reasons why, of all the moves that were made before, *these*
rather than others stuck. But such reasons do not seem to have a direct motivational
significance for the agents. More about this later.

tween soul and body re-created, not perhaps as a self-conscious philosophical project but, what makes it even more serious, as a recalcitrant datum that surfaces again and again, in spite of all the talk about integration and wholeness?

Perhaps. I don't want to deny that the view of human nature Montaigne will ultimately come up with is one in which *dis*integration and conflict have a dominating role, and I don't care to deny that words like "soul" or "body" could be used to designate some of the elements in conflict there. But I find it important to point out that the conflict is not to be located where the reconstruction suggested above would have it, that is, that the dividing line is not between (a concern with) the concrete, spatio-temporal world and (one with) the abstract, fictitious structures thought and language can conjure up. The dividing line, we know, has something to do with imagination and its laws, but "imagination" is still only a word—one that fools us more, the more our familiarity with it makes us think that we understand it. In order not to get fooled, we need to inquire deeper into the structure of this thing that—perhaps too quickly and unjustifiedly—we may have taken for granted.

Our fundamental text for this inquiry is a passage that comes immediately after the statement, quoted on p. 49, that "it is not easy to set limits to our mind." Here it is, in full:

> Having found by experience that where one man had failed, another has succeeded, and that what was unknown to one century the following century has made clear, and that the sciences and arts are not cast in a mold, but are formed and shaped little by little, by repeated handling and polishing, as the bears lick their cubs into shape at leisure, I do not leave off sounding and testing [*essayer*] what my powers cannot discover; and by handling again and kneading this new material, stirring it and heating it, I open up to whoever follows me some facility to enjoy it more at his ease, and make it more supple and manageable for him. (II 12, p. 421)

What is described here in some detail is precisely that activity of the mind to which "it is not easy to set limits": the activity of imagining new possibilities, of thinking of what has not been discovered yet and is not yet, therefore, part of accessible reality. But note how the activity operates. It is not that, when performing it, one stops moving in the ordinary world and recedes (or ascends) to a different, Platonic structure where bodily limitations are not going to impede one and concrete things occur at best as objects of discourse, hypothetical referents for an omnipotent, self-sufficient *logos*. Quite on the contrary, the description emphasizes *handling* as the key strategic element: the concrete, physical handling of some vaguely characterized "material." It would be easy to discount this emphasis as being metaphorical in nature, but for once let us resist the obvious and see where we can get by taking words at face value.

In this vein, a first suggestion the passage gives is that the activity in question is a *leisure* activity. It is not, in and by itself, a new suggestion: Aristotle already claimed that thought established its power—and realized man's full potential—only after certain peoples or classes had enough leisure to exercise it. The difference is in the context of the suggestion, and is, as we will see, a vast difference. For Aristotle believed that the power of thought—and man's potential—consisted in finding the true causes of things and events; with Montaigne the matter will have a less sanctimonious ring.

Second, there seems to be an affinity between this activity and play, in at least two, not unconnected, senses. The activity must give pleasure, or the analogy with the bears licking their cubs would be out of place. And the activity is performed for no direct (utilitarian) payoff. There is a vague, generic promise that performing it might be profitable in the end—just as playing might develop abilities that later, in adult life, prove useful to people.[13] But though that promise can have some impact in convincing one of the desirability of occasionally indulging in this activity, it cannot be what does the trick every individual time we proceed to so indulge. No, there is nothing definite to get at the end of it, so it must be the

---

[13] See I 25, p. 105, where, quoting approvingly from Agesilaus's words, Montaigne says that "children should learn . . . '[w]hat they should do when they are men.' "

pleasure intrinsic to the very moves that makes us do it, as is the case with the moves of running and chasing and ball handling.

Third, though the ultimate, distant point of the activity is declared to be the promotion of arts and sciences, its immediate outcome has to do with making something *softer*. The word used here is the same used in earlier quotes for the mind: "supple" (French: *soupple*). My hunch is that this is more than a coincidence, and that taking it seriously might tell us a lot of what "the mind" is.

No final resolution of the riddle can be reached until we know more about the material that is being handled and made softer. There is a fundamental ambiguity about the nature of this material that will have to be faced in the next section, but for the moment I suggest the following.[14] Suppose that what is handled here is exactly the same kind of thing that is handled during ordinary activities. Ordinarily, we might, for example, handle a chair: more specifically, say, *make* one according to instructions that come from an ancient, somewhat mysterious tradition and have been codified, more or less explicitly, in a sense (or a manual) of *style*. If for no other reason than that this methodology has become deeply entrenched for all of us chair makers, it is now most efficient to stick to it. Those moves have been imprinted in our muscles, we make them without choosing, without deliberating, without even thinking, which means: we make them most quickly and assuredly, without detours, without delay. But then one day we feel playful, we feel like doing something funny just for the sake of it. We might waste time in the process, but we do not care, we enjoy it so much. Thus we make a change in the ancient ritual: perhaps something apparently unimportant,[15] such as the order in which nails are driven into the wood, or perhaps something whose impact is devastating, say, the number of legs the chair has. Important or not, the change is bound to make us feel uneasy, insofar as we are breaking

[14] As the reader will see, this suggestion is in line with the previously expressed intention to resist a metaphorical reading of the passage.

[15] But beware: when variation is first allowed, no matter how small, it is difficult to stop (just as "it is a difficult thing to close a train of speech and cut it short once you are under way" [I 9, p. 22]).

old rules, contradicting established customs; but today we are ready to live with the uneasiness. In fact, the pleasure we take in doing what we are doing is no less for being hard-won; if anything, it is more. Now think of somebody who indulges constantly in this kind of behavior, who constantly plays with his hands and with the things around him, by moving his hands and those things in ways that are not codified (yet?), simply to see what comes, simply because he likes it. Isn't there a sense in which this person is *imagining* (details of) alternative worlds, not by talking about them but by having them take shape in front of him—imperfect, rudimentary shape probably, but shape nonetheless? And isn't there a sense in which he is breaking the stiffness that comes with habit, extending not only his but our freedom, giving us a chance to make our behavior less rigid, or softer?

The Stuff that Dreams Are Made Of

A possibility of recovering some level of integration between "mind" and "body" is now open to us. It is not that body lives in a world of things, and mind in a world of senses; rather, mind and body are two extremes in a continuum of interchange with and manipulation of one and the same reality, which it would be a mistake to call "physical" insofar as it is no less *mental*, in the new sense that "mental" is gradually coming to have for us. In this new sense, mind (or imagination) is the practice of doing violence to traditional moves, perhaps preliminary to establishing a new tradition, but not for the sake of such establishing—in fact, when the establishing has taken place, mind will continue its relentless, ruthless exploration beyond the new settlement. In this sense, the mind's operation is the importune, bold strategy of play: play with toys as much as with tools or institutions, the play that challenges old rituals and makes us look at things, or touch them, or place them, the "wrong" way, the play that is intrinsically transgression and perversion. And though there is a clear contrast between this liberating activity and the "bodily" one that proceeds blindfolded and fastened to the inevitability of custom, this is nothing but the contrast between two ways of handling the same material, the same "stuff." When seen along these lines, the "mind-body problem" evaporates, or at least reduces to the problem of understanding how one and the same person can put in a nine-to-five workday and then joyously explore carpentry, or fishing, or sex.[16]

But perhaps we went too far in promoting integration here. After all, Montaigne, though deeply interested in technological details and variants,[17] has no direct personal concern with them—at least not when he is involved in his philosophy, the activity we would most naturally associate with a mind. To do philosophy, he renounces all contact with the outside world, spending his time in a universe of words, surrounded by the books of his library, searching for appropriate quotes, rereading and glossing his (written) work. If this is play, some might object, it is intellectual play, if this is handling it is metaphorical handling, and how revealing—or even fair—is it to insist on taking the metaphor literally, and forcing the mental on the Procrustean bed of the desired "integration," when it would be so much easier to revert instead to the old scheme of things: a body that handles physical objects and a mind that thinks of—and possibly plays with—the senses of words?

Well, perhaps "easy" and "revealing" do not always make a good match; perhaps the fit we are looking for—Procrustean as it may be—will make us see things in ways that we will eventually find worth the trouble. At any rate, given how far we have followed our author already, it is reasonable to go one more step, and read one more quote:

> Handling and use by able minds give value to a language, not so much by innovating as by filling it out with more vigorous and varied services, by stretching and bending it. They do not

---

[16] Note an interesting analogy at III 5, p. 644, between books and sex (or better, sexual words): both "become all the more marketable and public by being suppressed." We have already noted the conflict between transgressive games and existing social values; in Chapter 6 we will explore the matter further.

[17] His *Travel Journal* is in this respect a precious mine of information. See pp. 871, 873, 881, 882, 887, 888, 896, 899, 902, 903, 910, 923, 931–32, 963, 999, 1030.

bring to it new words, but they enrich their own, give more weight and depth to their meaning and use; they teach the language unaccustomed movements, but prudently and shrewdly. (III 5, p. 665)

This prudent, gradual stretching, bending, and twisting of language is exactly what Montaigne is after.[18] It astonishes him, he says, "that those who engage in that business [of writing for the public] do not take it into their heads rather to choose ten thousand very beautiful stories that are found in books" than to make them up. If anyone were to follow this suggestion, "he would need to furnish only the connecting links of his own, like the solder of another metal" (II 35, p. 568). And Montaigne does follow the suggestion, and slowly but surely piles up one quote after another, one *existing* story after another, taking them out of their context and making a new context largely out of them, together with a few "connecting links" that he provides. This way, he teaches language "unaccustomed movements" by literally playing with it, and making it easier for others to do the same, making language a softer, more pliable, more supple tool.

Language—primarily as syntax[19]—is the material on which Montaigne's imagination operates: his dreams are verbal configurations,[20] his inventions are not new chairs, and not even "new words," but new verbal structures. Thus in the end we return to something much closer to the commonsensical view of this faculty, which we have been opposing most of the way: imagination is again the creation—or maybe just the modification—of stories. But we

[18] Note that at III 13, p. 816, where the use of language by learned men is compared with the handling of a mass of quicksilver by children (!), the same verb "to knead" (French: *pe[s]trisser*) is used as in the crucial passage quoted on p. 55.

[19] That is, primarily as it has a substance of its own, and does not resolve itself into the transparent reflection of something *else*.

[20] For this use of the word "dream," see II 12, pp. 354–55, where "the privilege in which our soul glories, of reducing to her condition all that she conceives, of stripping all that comes to her of its mortal and corporeal qualities, of constraining all the things that she considers worthy of her acquaintance to put off and divest themselves of their corruptible properties" is equated to the dreams of a horse, a greyhound, or a watchdog.

return to this characterization, quite appropriately, *in the end*. Our detour through the practical imagining of the player (the artist? the inventor?) makes us look at this characterization from a fresh, surprising angle.

For the commonsensical view, what matters in stories is what is being told—more precisely, the *sense* of what is being told. That the sense must be expressed and communicated through words, and that words retain a somewhat physical—though ethereal—nature, and do not follow their meanings away from this sublunar, imperfect reality, is probably due to our own imperfection, our own physical residue. Still, words are an occasion for transcendence, for a glimpse into what is not physical—with all the problems that relating the object of that glimpse *to* the physical will ultimately create. Uttering and manipulating words and verbal constructions is an occasion for grasping senses, and it is in order to grasp new senses that we need to utter and manipulate new words and constructions, to tell new stories. Imagination, or mind, or thought, is the faculty that makes it possible for us to extend the range of senses in our possession, and if this faculty is verbal, it is *accidentally* verbal: it would not be so if in grasping senses we were in the happy position of a mineralogist, who can put a crystal in the hands of his audience so that all can have a good *look* at it.[21]

For the view suggested by my reading of Montaigne, on the other hand, the notion of what words *mean*, of their senses, has no conceptual priority at all. If indeed it enters the picture, it must be at a relatively late conceptual stage, and one that we have no need to face here. What is conceptually prior, instead, is the notion of a practice: when it comes to mind, imagination, or thought, of a destabilizing, playful practice. The object of this practice can be any old object— and let us say *physical* object in order to be understood, even though in the new picture I am drawing the difference between physical and mental suggested by this qualification is bound eventually to ex-

---

[21] The obvious reference here is to Frege's "Thoughts," p. 360, footnote. For a more specific criticism of these themes in the philosophy of language, see my "A New Paradigm of Meaning."

plode.[22] It can also be language; in fact, for reasons that we will go into later, it may prove especially convenient that it be language, so convenient that it turns out to be language most of the time. But if it is language, it is language precisely insofar as language is like any old object: not, that is, insofar as there is something *beyond* language, a reality that is different from all we can see and touch and that is bound to remain inaccessible in its purest form but that language somehow puts us in communication with—though veiling it and distorting it at the same time. No, it is language insofar as it has a texture just like tables and chairs, insofar as it offers resistance like them, insofar as we can see it and hear it, and stretch and bend and twist what we see and hear. It is language insofar as it is part of our behavior, part of our codified, structured moves, and insofar as— like anything else that is codified and structured—violence can be done to it.

[22] In *Kant's Copernican Revolution* I discuss in some detail the problem and the difficulties of communicating across different conceptual schemes.

CHAPTER FIVE

MADNESS AND METHOD

"O man," said that God [at Delphi], ". . . you are the
investigator without knowledge, the magistrate
without jurisdiction, and all in all, the fool of
the farce."
(III 9, p. 766)

಼

Trivial Pursuits

THERE ARE THREE kinds of desires, Montaigne says (rehearsing a
well-known Epicurean line). Some are natural and necessary, some
natural and not necessary, and some neither natural nor necessary.
"Of this last type," he adds, "are nearly all those of men; they are
all superfluous and artificial" (II 12, p. 346).[1] It is "marvelous"
(ibid.) how little our nature really needs, and how much of what we
want we could do without. Marvelous indeed, so much so as to
invite questions on the origin and significance (if any) of this discrepancy.

To those who would ask such questions, Montaigne answers
with the sketch of a quasi-psychological theory that has since become associated with a long tradition of political thinkers, at least
from Rousseau on. Here is a formulation of it: "Thus men ruin

[1] See also III 10, p. 771: "When the sages tell us that according to Nature no one
is indigent and that everyone is so according to opinion, they distinguish subtly between the desires that come from her and those that come from the disorder of our
imagination; in this way: those whose limits we can see are hers, those that flee before
us and whose end we cannot reach are ours." The role of imagination will come to
the fore shortly.

63

themselves by letting themselves become entangled in restricting regimens, and by superstitiously tying themselves down to them. They still need more, and still more after that; it is never done" (III 13, p. 847).

Generalizing on the sickness-and-cure horizon within which (as so often in Montaigne) this statement is confined, the line is a familiar one. We start out trying something—a tool, a diet, or whatever—that promises to, and perhaps does, for the moment, make our life easier. Then, possibly because our life *is* in fact made easier, we indulge in it more and more, we get used to it, and finally we become dependent on it. By the end of the process, our life is no longer easier: we are now weaker beings who can expect nothing but a much needed relief from addiction, not real pleasure, from our new toy.[2] "[L]ike those who by artificial light extinguish the light of day, we have extinguished our own means by borrowed means" (I 36, p. 167). And the net result is that "Nature . . . a gentle guide, but no more gentle than wise and just" has been corrupted, and "her footprints . . . confused . . . with artificial tracks" (III 13, p. 855): "[I]n us [her laws] are lost" (II 12, p. 438).

Consistently with this diagnosis, Montaigne shuns all artificial remedies. "[W]hen I am sick," he says, "what nature cannot do for me, I do not want to have done by a pill" (III 9, p. 751). Better to resist the fascination of what presents itself thus, with a benevolent smile; for remember that "clemency and magnanimity . . . [are] excellent lures to attract men" (*Letter* 37, p. 1092), and that they frequently issue in conquests more thorough than what could be obtained by arms and force. The conclusion of a man who has devoted such a considerable time and attention to the preservation of his

---

[2] See I 14, p. 40 ("we have corrupted our soul with shaded ease, luxuries, idleness, languor, sloth; we have softened it by evil opinions and habits [quoted from Cicero]"); II 12, p. 335 ("the excess and unruliness of our appetite [outstrip] all the inventions with which we seek to satisfy it"). See also III 6, p. 690, for an interesting parallelism with the situation of a liberal king: "[T]he more [he] exhausts himself in giving, the poorer he makes himself in friends. How could he assuage desires that grow the more they are fulfilled?" (In the last chapter, the analogy with a king will become crucial.)

own health, so much indeed as to bring him to observe, mortified, "It is a stupid habit to keep count of what you piss" (*Travel Journal*, p. 988), is entirely on the side of simple, and sometimes cruel, Nature: "There is no other medicine, no other rule or science, for avoiding the ills, whatever they may be and however great, that besiege men from all sides and at every hour, than to make up our minds to suffer them humanly, or to end them courageously and promptly" (ibid., p. 1018).

But what lures are these? Where does this dangerous fascination ultimately issue from? Unmistakably, it bears the marks of that counterfactual, destabilizing agency that we variously designated as "mind," "reason," and "imagination." After all, how could we even relate to something other than current, blind, repetitive practice if we did not experiment with alternative possibilities, with nonactual courses of events? How could the (deceptive?) promise of a better, easier, healthier life even become an issue for us if we were not able to somehow picture it to ourselves, by words, by images, or by the simple play of our hands? Without the "degree of freedom" thus made possible, there would be nothing but the unconscious efficiency of habit, of the one habit we are born in, and no chance of developing other, "artificial" needs or wants. Thus, dialectically, such freedom turns against itself, and is exposed as the true cause of our worst slavery: the slavery *we* are responsible for. "Much thanks to our sickly, kill-joy mind, which disgusts us with [natural pleasures] as well as with itself. It treats both itself and all that it takes in, whether future or past, according to its insatiable, erratic, and versatile nature" (III 13, p. 849). And as an obvious counterpart to this evil, there emerges an ideal of mythical simplicity: "The more simply we trust to Nature, the more wisely we trust to her. Oh, what a sweet and soft and healthy pillow is ignorance and incuriosity, to rest a well-made head!" (ibid., p. 822).[3]

---

[3] See also II 12, pp. 404–405, where "the cannibals" are said to "enjoy the happiness of a long, tranquil, and peaceable life without the precepts of Aristotle and without acquaintance with the name of physics," whereas philosophers "have renounced" the natural state and hence can no longer appeal to it. At I 54, p. 227, Montaigne says

Such antirationalistic pronouncements are a common (if controversial) outcome of this whole line of thought. In Montaigne, they are occasionally quite extreme. Thus, not only are "the lofty and exquisite ideas of philosophy . . . found to be inept in practice" (II 20, p. 511), not only do "[t]hat acute vivacity of mind, that supple and restless versatility, [disturb] our negotiations" (ibid.): there are problems, and serious ones, even with less lofty, more down-to-earth forms of awareness. A clear, suggestive statement to this effect is made by Montaigne through the use of an apologue (II 37, pp. 591-92). The inhabitants of the region of Lahontan "lived a life apart, . . . ruled and governed by certain particular systems and customs, handed down from father to son, to which they bound themselves with no other constraint than that of reverence for their practice." As a result, they were "in so happy a condition that no neighboring judge had been put to the trouble of inquiring into their doings, no lawyer retained to give them counsel, no foreigner ever called in to settle their quarrels; and no one . . . had ever been seen begging." All this until "one of them . . . took it into his head . . . to make one of his sons . . . into a fine village notary." Immediately, the whole business of trials and judges entered that happy place, and debased it; immediately, people became litigious and nasty. Nor did misfortunes end there. A doctor married one of the girls and settled in the district.

> He first began to teach them the names of fevers, colds, and abscesses, the situation of the heart, liver, and intestines, . . . [and they] swear that only since then they noticed that the night air made them heavy-headed, that drinking when they were heated was harmful, and that autumn winds were more unhealthy than those of spring; that since they have used medicine they find themselves overwhelmed with a legion of un-

---

that "for [his] part [he] draw[s] back as much as [he] can into the first and natural stage, which for naught [he] attempted to leave." (But we know already that his values are not as straightforward as that, and later we will inquire why.)

accustomed illnesses; and that they perceive a general decline in their former vigor, and their lives cut short by half.

In other words, novelty and curiosity are nothing but a source of trouble. If a new remedy cures anything, it is likely to cure what it itself caused in the first place.[4]

I said that pronouncements of this kind are fairly common, and that they are controversial. The main reason for the latter is that they seem to rely on a serious ambiguity, and consequently have to face an equally serious criticism. Take the pill issue. I won't take a pill, Montaigne says, because I want to rely on what is natural. At first, the justification seems to make sense; but when we put some pressure on it, it collapses. Why, isn't a pill nature? Isn't it made of natural elements, and isn't it because of its natural properties that it has whatever beneficial effect we—rightly or wrongly—attribute to it? And in general, how do we decide that it is unnatural, or supernatural or antinatural, for us to use a tool of any sort instead of—or in addition to—our hands and feet and other body parts? After all, some animals use tools, too:

> When bulls go into combat, they spread and toss the dust around them; boars whet their tusks; and the ichneumon, when he is to come to grips with the crocodile, arms his body, coats it, and crusts it all over with mud, well pressed and well kneaded, as with a cuirass. Why shall we not say that it is just as natural to arm ourselves with wood and iron? (II 12, p. 335)

And the answer is: we shall. "[T]he skill to fortify and protect the body by acquired means, we possess by a natural instinct and precept" (ibid.).

---

[4] In *Travel Journal*, p. 1021, "one very elderly man" is reported as saying that "for a number of years he had observed that the baths [at La Villa] did more harm than good to those who used them," and that "the cause of it was this: that whereas in times past there was not a single apothecary in these parts, and you never saw a doctor except rarely, now you see the contrary." At III 13, p. 816, we are told that "lawyers and doctors are a bad provision for a country" because they make "our common language, so easy for any other use, . . . obscure and unintelligible" and because, "[b]y sowing questions and cutting them up, they make the world fructify and teem with uncertainty and quarrels."

There is more to Nature than the earlier simplistic suggestions might have led one to believe, and Montaigne knows it very well. He knows that "nature enfolds within the bounds of her ordinary progress, like all other things, also the beliefs, judgments, and opinions of men" (ibid., p. 433), that "no great desire can be imagined that is so strange and vicious that nature is not involved in it" (III 13, p. 833), and that even the destabilizing "desire for knowledge" is such that "[t]here is no desire more natural than [it]" (ibid., p. 815). He knows—or better, fears—that there is even "some instinct for inhumanity" that "Nature . . . attaches to man" (II 11, p. 316). Those earlier references were ideological, they threw a value-ridden word such as "Nature" on one extreme of a spectrum of *natural* developments, and the result, implicitly, was a value judgment and an ethical command: do not follow mind away from the beaten path, do not leave home, do not ask too many questions. We have already seen that Montaigne does not always obey the command, and we know that, possibly for this reason, he has no high opinion of himself; but before we turn to such moral issues, we need to address a factual query, which is nothing but a reformulation, in the new vocabulary and against the wider background introduced here, of a familiar perplexity. Why is man so naturally led to artificiality? Why does the structure of his needs and desires *naturally* develop into something ever more complex? Why, if those needs and desires could be so much more easily stunted than satisfied, and nobody (apparently) would be the worse for it? What is the point of this empty pursuit?

Child's Play

The analogy between mental activity and games has already become part of our discourse.[5] Both elude any straightforward utilitarian

---

[5] See pp. 56–57 above.

analysis in terms of the achievement of some goal;[6] both are characterized by a higher level of freedom than ordinary, everyday kinds of concerns. Indeed, the philosopher often matches the child in his forgetfulness of social conventions and his troublesome, limpid cry that the king is naked. "Aristippus said that the chief fruit he had gathered from philosophy was that he spoke freely and openly to everyone" (II 17, p. 492), and Montaigne is not going to be more cautious: he will give himself up "to being candid and always saying what [he thinks], by inclination and by reason, leaving it to Fortune to guide the outcome" (ibid.).

Play and philosophy, I suggested, have also another aspect in common: they cause pleasure. Socrates, the archetypal philosopher, whose attitude is "childlike" (III 12, p. 807), has a "serene and smiling" expression, "not settled like that of old Crassus, who was never seen to laugh" (III 5, p. 641). And what he invites us to is gay, "a gay and sociable wisdom" (ibid.; see also III 13, p. 857), so much so that—contrary to popular misconceptions— children would enjoy it.

It is very wrong to portray [philosophy] as inaccessible to children, with a surly, frowning, and terrifying face. Who has masked her with this false face, pale and hideous? There is nothing more gay, more lusty, more sprightly, and I might almost say more frolicsome. She preaches nothing but merrymaking and a good time. A sad and dejected look shows that she does not dwell there. (I 26, p. 118)[7]

The analogy thus belabored has more than mere taxonomical significance; like all taxonomies, it holds a promise of explanation. It was at this explanation that I hinted when I said in the preceding chapter that the (vague, distant) point of mental trickery might be

---

[6] At the end of the present analysis, it would be possible to understand its results in terms of *rule* utilitarianism. But I am not the first to notice that rule utilitarianism may be teleological only by name.

[7] See also ibid., p. 120 ("Since it is philosophy that teaches us to live, and since there is a lesson in it for childhood as well as for the other ages, why is it not imparted to children?"); II 17, p. 483 ("I do not love a solemn and gloomy wisdom, as does the world").

of the same sort as that of playing: to help us "develop abilities that later, in adult life, prove useful to people." Which, ultimately, might also account for the pleasure associated with both kinds of games: if those abilities are indeed useful, it is to be expected that—as in the case of nutrition or reproduction—the practice of learning them be accompanied by some "positive reinforcement." "Nature has observed this principle like a mother, that the actions she has enjoined on us for our need should also give us pleasure; and she invites us to them not only through reason, but also through appetite" (III 13, p. 850).

Several of Montaigne's statements go along with this suggestion, for example when he notes that "children's games are not games, and must be judged in children like their more serious actions" (I 23, p. 79).[8] There the context makes it clear that he thinks of child's play as being primarily a school of life, one in which man's character is built, as are, presumably, his skills, and hence one that mirrors his future inclinations and concerns. Nor is this kind of schooling to end when childhood is over: in adult age, play continues under the guise of thought, where (as we have seen) a constant confrontation is staged with what is not but might, and possibly will, be. There are limits to how far this intellectual game can match reality, for "athwart all our plans, counsels and precautions, Fortune still maintains her grasp on the results" (I 24, p. 92),[9] and even our own reactions are hardly predictable: "I have little control over myself and my moods. Chance has more power here than I. The occasion, the company, the very sound of my voice, draw more from my mind than I find in it when I sound it and use it by myself" (I 10, p.

---

[8] See also footnote 13 of Chapter 4.

[9] See also I 47, p. 209 ("events and outcomes depend for the most part, especially in war, on Fortune, who will not fall into line and subject herself to our reason and foresight"); II 4, p. 263 ("But when all is said, it is hard in human actions to arrive by reasoning at any rule so exact as to exclude Fortune from her rights in the matter"); III 8, p. 713 ("It is unwise to think that human wisdom can fill the role of Fortune"). At I 32, p. 159, an interesting wrinkle is added: reasoning is a way of "combating" things, and is especially weak with "things unknown" which thus become "[t]he true field and subject of imposture."

26).[10] But if awareness of these limits inclines Montaigne "to modesty, obedience to the beliefs that are prescribed [him], a constant coolness and moderation in [his] opinions, and . . . hatred for that aggressive and quarrelsome arrogance that believes and trusts wholly in itself" (III 13, p. 823), if indeed such awareness brings him to be "so made that [he] like[s] as well to be lucky as wise" (III 10, p. 784), still in all modesty the game can continue, working toward that wisdom which promises to anticipate the fact and thereby bring about "an orderly management of our soul" (II 2, p. 251). The promise may be largely delusive, but it will be *less* delusive if we take it seriously, if we insist on playing the game right, with all the earnest intensity it requires,[11] if we constantly keep in focus its practical significance and check the tendency to become lost in it. When the latter happens, as is often the case in chess, one's attitude is no longer childlike, but "puerile" (I 50, p. 220): "I hate [chess] and avoid it, because it is not enough a game, and too serious an amusement; I am ashamed to devote to it the attention that would suffice to accomplish something good" (ibid.).

On these conditions the game of thought can really become, with all its weaknesses, an important source of new strategies, a laboratory for future behavior:

> [Etienne de la Boétie] interrupted me . . . to show in action
> that the talks we had had together during our health had been
> not merely borne in our mouths but deeply engraved on heart

---

[10] Nor would it be enough to predict, since practical moves have a way of eluding rational control anyhow: "A man whose thoughts are elsewhere will not fail, to the inch, to take always the same number and length of steps in the place where he walks; but if he goes at it attentively, measuring and counting them, he will find that what he did naturally and by chance, he will not do as exactly by design" (II 17, p. 493; see also III 1, p. 603).

[11] Note that playing this game right will also include being subjectively convinced of its value—in spite of all our talk of its defects and limitations. This conflict of interests is a first basis for Montaigne's surprising statements in favor of erratic minds: see the passage from II 37, p. 580, quoted on p. 37 above, and also, for example, I 39, p. 179 ("I *cannot believe* that . . . the effects of reason cannot match the effects of habit" [italics mine]). More motivation for such statements will emerge later.

and in soul, in such a way as to be put into execution on the first occasions that offered; *adding that this was the true object of our studies, and of philosophy.* (*Letter 2*, p. 1051; italics mine)[12]

And note that the intensity and the earnestness do not exclude the possibility that this later apprenticeship will continue to bear the marks of enjoyment and fun. "[W]hat I have begun to say in sport and in jest," we are told, "I will say seriously the next day" (III 5, p. 668), and "[i]f anyone tells me that it is degrading the Muses to use them only as a plaything and a pastime, he does not know, as I do, the value of pleasure, play, and pastime. I would almost say that any other aim is ridiculous" (III 3, p. 629).

But perhaps we went too fast. For one thing, what is the point of Socrates' childlike and gamesome attitude *in front of death*? What new strategy was he practicing *then*, with time running out on him? We may think of a mechanism gone crazy, of a tic reiterating itself long after its point was lost, but then why does Montaigne *applaud* such behavior?[13] Furthermore, what about Montaigne's *own* behavior? He might not like chess, but consider the single-minded dedication that—as we know from Chapter 1—he shows for the exploration of the most minute aspects of himself. Consider his craving for travel, consider his many statements against ethnocentrism, consider his "sickness for freedom." Can we account for all of this as a kind of training? A training for what? The man has already passed his prime; at times he seems to think that he has already lived longer than he should have.[14]

There are passages where Montaigne suggests that exercise is valuable in itself, independently of any payoff. Thus philosophers, he reminds us approvingly, "did not think it inappropriate to exercise

---

[12] See also II 36, p. 569, where Homer's books are regarded "as a nursery of every kind of ability."

[13] See, for example, I 14, p. 34.

[14] See I 57, p. 237; III 9, p. 750; III 13, p. 845. At I 57, p. 238, Montaigne says "we should not allot so great a part of [our life] to birth, idleness, and apprenticeship," and at II 28 (an essay significantly entitled "All Things Have Their Season"), p. 531, he judges that "[w]hat they tell of [Cato the Censor] among other things, that in his extreme old age he set himself to learn Greek with an ardent appetite, as if to quench a long thirst, does not seem to me to be much in his honor. It is exactly what we call falling back into childhood."

and amuse their minds on things in which there was no solid profit" (II 12, p. 377). Nor is it just a matter of a disinterested quest for *truth*, as the current ideology often goes: "[T]hey exercised their minds on such conceptions as had at least a pleasant and subtle appearance, provided that, *false though they might be*, they could hold their own against opposing ideas" (ibid., p. 379; italics mine). Where a major arena for this kind of practice for practice's sake seems to be the written word: "Books," Montaigne says, "have served me not so much for instruction as for exercise" (III 12, p. 795).

But to say that exercise is an end in itself is the same as saying that it has no end, or that we do not know which end it has, if any. Ultimately, this may be the reason why Montaigne finds himself, as we have seen, "full of inanity and nonsense" (III 9, p. 766), indeed, why he thinks that man in general "feeds on inanity and is subject to its power" (III 4, p. 638): because man is "but sedition and discrepancy" (III 5, p. 659), because his condition is "so hostile to consistency" (III 9, p. 758), because "we are, I know not how, double within ourselves, with the result that we do not believe what we believe, and we cannot rid ourselves of what we condemn" (II 16, p. 469). Once again,[15] there surfaces a kind of schizophrenia, this time generalized to the whole human tribe, and hence, if health is what we said—a function of the integration and the syntonic working of the whole organism—then it is legitimate to conclude that "[w]e are never without sickness" (II 12, p. 428). For what else shall we call this urge to prepare ourselves for what is not there—even when it is clear that, were it ever to *get* there, *we* will no longer be? What else shall we call this investment of time and energy, in clear defiance of all principles of economy and thrift, and with no hope of a dividend that justifies the risk? Sickness, we should call it, or madness: we are but the fools of the farce.

Montaigne's bewildering mixture of ultraconservatism and radicalism has been an issue all along. The analogy with play promised to resolve the issue: we need solid habits to fall back on, and room

---

[15] See p. 42 above, where a schizophrenic element was identified in Montaigne's own behavior.

to experiment freely—as a prelude to the formation of new, even more efficient habits. But, apparently, the promise was short-lived: none of us needs, or can implement, that many habits, none of us has the time, so why bother? It is natural to think that something has gone awry; it is natural to invoke abnormality of one sort or another. And again, we feel that this cannot be the whole story, at least as far as Montaigne goes. For what shall we think of his re-peated statements that "our wisdom [is] less wise than madness" (ibid., p. 427), or that "the subtlest madness [is] made . . . [of] the subtlest wisdom" (ibid., p. 363)? How shall we assess the fact that after claiming he is "much afraid that we shall have very greatly hastened the decline and ruin of this new world [that is, America] by our contagion" (III 6, p. 693), and irremediably infected with our sickness an "infant" environment (ibid.) whose purity, simplicity, and naturalness should have been left alone, put away and cherished as sacred, [16] that after all this earnest preaching he should proceed to ridicule those who "travel covered and wrapped in a taciturn and incommunicative prudence, defending themselves from the conta-gion [!] of an unknown atmosphere" (III 9, p. 754)? Is the contagion of diversity and novelty a value, a danger, or what? [17]

Perhaps we should just forget about Montaigne: *he* is but sedition and discrepancy, and a fool. Or perhaps not. Perhaps we are not looking at this thing the right way, and there is another point of view that needs to be brought in before it can all begin to make sense.

Variations on the World Theme

Within the apparent confusion of Montaigne's statements, a few things remain clear. First, his value judgments are all in favor of the

[16] See also I 30, p. 146: "As if our touch were infectious, we by our handling corrupt things that of themselves are beautiful and good."

[17] An additional complication here is the following: even *as a danger*, this contagion has some value. Consider for example the following passage: "[T]he towns . . . are undoubtedly strengthened and further joined and united by the impact of the neigh-boring [religious] contagion" (*Travel Journal*, p. 885).

community: childlike and gamesome as he may have been, "the great and good Socrates" is to be admired primarily because he "refused to save his life by disobedience to the magistrate, even to a very unjust and very iniquitous magistrate" (I 23, p. 86). And even when trouble strikes closer to home, even "in the strife that is tearing France to pieces," where "[t]he justest party is still a member of a worm-eaten and maggoty body," even there "[w]e may regret better times, but not escape the present; we may wish for different magistrates, but we must nevertheless obey those that are here. And perhaps there is more merit in obeying the bad than the good" (III 9, p. 760). Second, the revolutionary practices of the mind are intrinsically individualistic in nature. They result in putting customs—even possible customs—one against the other, and consequently weakening their hold; they follow personal inclinations (to travel, to read) away from the cast imposed by rigid, traditional rules, and toward the formation of a life experience that is unique in character, and absolutely original at least in the "connecting links" that it provides for the patches it works on—a life experience in which one can take *personal* pride. Third, these practices, these "essays," these "studies," perverse as they may be, have a function, a "true object," which is to be conceived in terms of some kind of training. Given their individualistic orientation, it is natural to conclude that—if they are to be functional at all—they must be functional *to the individual*, and hence result in training *the individual* to something that will turn out to be useful *to him*. And here we come to a stall, since the individual has often no use for what he thus "learns." "All the ability of ours that is beyond the natural is as good as vain and superfluous," Montaigne says, and "[i]t is a lot if it does not load us down and bother us more than it serves us" (III 12, p. 794). But suppose now that the conclusion above is not at all intended: suppose that the agency favored by the value judgments— the *locus* of values—is also the point of view from which issues of functionality must be decided. Suppose that the functions the individualistic wanderings of mind perform are relevant not to the individual but to the community. Can that be? Can something that appears to be designed for a certain purpose end up systematically serving a different, indeed an antagonistic, master?

We are not like the happy inhabitants of Lahontan. Perhaps nobody is; perhaps even if the boy never went to school, and the doctor never married into the district, something else would have happened. Perhaps no district can be protected from contagion indefinitely, and no environment will, in the long run, resist mixing with foreign viruses that attempt to corrupt its integrity. Perhaps it is best to do something before that time comes: *play* with viruses, get ready for them.

Reason, we know, is the theater of restless variations, but the world we experience is no steady state. If the former "has so many shapes that we know not which to lay hold of," the latter "has no fewer," and hence "[t]he inference that we try to draw from the resemblance of events is uncertain, because they are always dissimilar: there is no quality so universal in this aspect of things as diversity and variety" (III 13, p. 815).[18] Nor are we in a position to tell when diversity is going to hit: we may live for centuries in a safe haven like Lahontan and then, suddenly, for reasons that could not be anticipated—or such that, had they been anticipated, we would not have taken them seriously—find ourselves at a loss, facing a situation that we have no way of handling.

What makes things even worse is the specific way humans function. We know from Chapter 2 that it is not enough for them to be told *about* what they should do. The moves a given task requires must be written in more than books: they must be written in our muscles and nerves, they must be part *of us*. True, as "circumstances and things roll about and change incessantly," we might derive

---

[18] See also I 26, p. 116 ("whoever reads such universal and constant variety in [Nature's] face . . . that man alone estimates things according to their true proportions"); II 2, p. 244 ("The world is nothing but variety and dissimilarity"); II 12, p. 455 ("all mortal things go on flowing and rolling unceasingly"); III 3, p. 621 ("Life is an uneven, irregular, and multiform movement"); III 13, p. 840 ("There is great uncertainty, variety, and obscurity about what [Nature] promises us or threatens us with"). Occasionally, the comparison between the unruliness of Nature and that of reason is drawn explicitly (as in the last passage quoted in the text): see I 47, p. 209 ("Fortune . . . involves our reason also in her confusion and uncertainty"), and II 12, p. 383 ("Fortune herself is no more diverse and variable than our reason, nor more blind and unthinking").

some hope from the fact that "[t]here are secret parts in the matters we handle which cannot be guessed, especially in human nature— mute factors that do not show, factors sometimes unknown to their possessor himself, which are brought forth and aroused by unex- pected occasions" (III 2, p. 618); but we cannot leave it at that, or we would be too dependent on chance and luck. Luck must be helped, those mute factors must be cultivated before they become relevant, somebody must have developed the right reactions before they are even right. And how can that be? How can humans, who are most effective when they respond blindly and automatically to the existing environment, remain effective while they worry about what does not (yet) exist, and train for it?

I suspect that what is emerging here may be the strongest argu- ment there is for the *social* character of human nature; not, that is, for why man *is* a social animal, but for why he *should* be, why there *should* be "nothing to which nature seems to have inclined us more than to society" (I 28, p. 136), why it should be true that (in the words of Plato's lawgiver) "neither are you your own nor is what you enjoy your own," but "[b]oth your goods and yourselves be- long to your family, past as well as future," and "even more do both your family and your goods belong to the public" (II 8, pp. 289– 90).[19]

Try to imagine what it would be like if individuals were self-suf- ficient and isolated: each of them might be perfectly integrated within the biotope, but if the biotope changed beyond the individ- uals' capacity for adaptation, then each and every one of them would become obsolete. There is of course a chance that biology has already provided some mutants that are ready to rise to the un- expected occasion, but it is only a chance, and one that was already missed many times: ask the dinosaurs. On the other hand, consider

[19] See also III 9, p. 730: "[H]uman society holds and is knit together at any cost whatever. Whatever position you set men in, they pile up and arrange themselves by moving and crowding together, just as ill-matched objects, put in a bag without order, find of themselves a way to unite and fall into place together, often better than they could have been arranged by art."

what it *is* like: in the present state of affairs, individuals divide their labor among themselves and become dependent on one another in subtle, intricate ways. Thus, even in the same general environment, they are going to internalize different behavioral programs, different sets of automatic responses, each adequate to the task it has been assigned. And this opens more than a capacity for variation: it also opens a possibility of dealing with future disturbing agents. For some will make shoes, some will make cars, and some . . . some may even feed on inanity and nonsense.

"Shall we then dare to say that . . . reason . . . has been put in us for our torment?" (I 14, pp. 36–37) By now, we begin to see how we can flesh out the required negative answer to this rhetorical question. The "error" of "always gaping after future things," if indeed we "dare to call an error something to which Nature herself leads us in serving the continuation of her work," that error by which "[w]e are never at home, we are always beyond" (I 3, p. 8), has a point after all: "philosophy, . . . as the molder of judgment and conduct, . . . has this privilege of being *everywhere at home*" (I 26, pp. 121–22; italics mine). So this is how the deviant, supple, mad mental concern with the unreal can be made "consistent with divine justice and forethought, which should guide all things toward utility" (III 13, p. 835). Habit "can shape us not only into whatever form it pleases . . . , but also shape us for change and variation, *which is the noblest and most useful of its teachings*" (ibid., p. 830; italics mine). For his part, we know, Montaigne thinks that the best of his bodily qualities is that he is "flexible and not very stubborn," and he invites all young men to follow his example and violate their own rules, in order to "arouse [their] vigor and keep it from growing moldy and lax" (ibid.).[20] It is natural to understand this statement, at first, as referring to the private pleasure of an individual who maintains a high level of adrenaline and feels the vital juices flow forcefully through his body, but then this reading could not explain what is "most useful" about shaping for change, or even less what

[20] See footnote 15 of Chapter 3 and the attending text.

is "noblest" about it. These adjectives make sense if we move to a higher level of analysis and understand the significance of variation as relevant not to the individual but to the community, insofar as when the *context* varies the community has thus maximized the pool of potential candidates to deal with the *new* context. This explanation does not deny that the individual experiences a private pleasure in being run through by fiery juices, or that the reason he "violates his own rules" is this private pleasure. We know how tricky Nature is. How many of us lovemakers make love *in order to* have children? Or, if you will, how often?

The argument is a complicated one, so I will summarize it. The preservation of life and health is the ultimate, decisive goal.[21] Achievement of this goal requires establishing an effective set of responses to the environment, and this in turn requires as much training as necessary to make those responses into blind and automatic routine. Such training will deaden most of the individual's potentialities, and exalt and refine only those whose actualization proves immediately useful. But we have no control on the environment: it may change dramatically, and our routines may become outdated. On the other hand, training all individuals for all possible developments of the environment may result in utter lack of effectiveness. So, whereas "[o]ur principal talent is the ability to apply ourselves to various practices" (III 3, p. 621), there is a limit to how much variety each of us can tolerate and still function. At this point, community comes to the rescue. Let us have a few superfluous individuals—superfluous for the purposes presently at hand—train for what is *not* at hand, and perhaps never *will* be at hand, but *could* be at hand. Let us have those individuals spend their time *playing*, which is to say: spreading the practices all over the map, following

---

[21] At II 8, p. 279, Montaigne says that, in his opinion, "the affection that the begetter has for his begotten ranks second," as an "instinct that is seen universally and permanently imprinted in both the animals and ourselves . . . , after the care every animal has for its own preservation and the avoidance of what is harmful." The latter care, then, must rank first.

them wherever they go, exploring the most remote possibilities of action. The chances are that most of this time and effort will be wasted, that most of these routes will turn into blind alleys, and that the childlike pleasure the players feel will be only puerile, but so it is with every form of insurance; isn't it?[22]

[22] This summary may be regarded as attributing to Montaigne a quasi-evolutionistic account of the mental (and other) components of human nature, and this attribution may then sound like an anachronism. To avoid confusion, I want to specify that, though I have no objection to the term "quasi-evolutionistic," the weight of the "quasi" is considerable. For, aside from the mathematical machinery and the experimental basis of evolution theory, which clearly does not belong in this context (unless we want to call "experimental" the basis that Montaigne finds for his claims in other written—indeed, literary—texts), there is no hint here of the mechanism of natural selection. As stated in the present summary (and argued in this chapter and the preceding ones), Montaigne limits himself to attributing some utility to all human (and animal) traits, and finding the specific utility of mental "deviation" in its capacity to match the variability of Nature by anticipating it to some extent. If this position is considered quasi-evolutionistic, so be it; but note that it is perfectly compatible with there being no evolution at all. What it commits one to is only the thesis that a "suppler" kind of being will in general function better than a more rigid one in an environment as unpredictable as ours is.

CHAPTER SIX

BLEAK EXPECTATIONS

And if it is true that [man] alone of all the animals has
this freedom of imagination and this unruliness in
thought . . . , it is an advantage that is sold him very
dear, and in which he has little cause to glory.

(II 12, p. 336)

❧

Crime and Punishment

OUR WANDERINGS have left us—or, if you will, left man—in a no-win situation. On the one hand, the community is the seat of values: if the supreme goal is health, and health is a matter of integration and coordinated work, then such integration and coordination do not stop at the level of the individual.[1] The individual is educated through example and training to reiterate the practices of his predecessors. The rules of custom are inscribed in his muscles and nerves, and with them comes a horror, repentine as it is beneficial, for whatever is new, strange, or foreign—a horror that is the first, mysterious, but authoritative source of all moral judgment. On the other hand, the very survival of the community requires that some of its members play with fire,[2] that they experiment with the un-

---

[1] Nor, for that matter, *could* they stop at this level, at least for the reason given in the preceding section and rehearsed below. Which means, among other things, that there is more interconnection between the two horns of the present dilemma than one might think.

[2] At III 12, p. 807, Montaigne says that Socrates "owed his life not to himself but to the world as an example. Would it not be a public loss if he had finished it in an idle and obscure fashion?"

heard and the uncanny, that they challenge and break the rules of tradition. In the void of established conventions in which they will operate,[3] these unfortunate guinea pigs will risk more than their life and limb: they will waste their own integrity and expose themselves to shame. "We regard our being as vice" (III 5, p. 670), Montaigne says, and for a good reason: because "[m]an ordains that he himself shall be necessarily at fault" (III 9, p. 758).[4]

Thus, there is inevitable guilt connected with the human condition, and specifically, with the activity that is most human of all and more than any other makes it possible for us to develop that "principal talent" of ours, "the ability to apply ourselves to various practices." I am referring, of course, to the activity of imagination, or reason, the activity of doubting and testing and essaying; I am referring to philosophy, or to whatever we want to call what Montaigne does and what Socrates and others did before him. "I am content . . . to live a merely excusable life," Montaigne says. But on the very next page, discussing the eighteen years he has been managing an estate, he judges his attitude as being one of "inexcusable [!] and childish laziness and negligence" (ibid., pp. 727–28).[5] Childish indeed, as philosophy is supposed to be, but also unprofessional and irresponsible: "What would I not do rather than read a contract, rather than go and disturb those dusty masses of papers . . . ? Nothing costs me dear except care and trouble, and I seek only to grow indifferent and relaxed" (ibid.).

"Cicero says that to philosophize is nothing else but to prepare for death" (I 20, p. 56), and Montaigne lists two possible reasons for this opinion. The second one sounds fairly standard (though see below): "[A]ll the wisdom and reasoning in the world boils down finally . . . to teach us not to be afraid to die" (ibid.). But the first one is newer and more suggestive, and may be worth closer atten-

---

[3] But see the discussion on philosophy as an institution at the very end of this chapter.

[4] See also I 50, p. 221 ("it seems to me that we can never be despised as much as we deserve"); III 5, p. 669 ("Perhaps we are right to blame ourselves for making such a stupid production as man, to call the [sexual] action shameful, and shameful the parts that are used for it").

[5] See also II 17, p. 488.

tion. "[S]tudy and contemplation," Montaigne says, "draw our soul out of us to some extent and keep it busy outside the body; which is a sort of apprenticeship and semblance of death" (ibid.). There is affinity between the ways philosophy and death work, and if this passage still leaves us somewhat in the dark as to the exact nature of the affinity by using the cipher alphabet of "soul" and "body," we may now be in a position to decode the message a little better.

Death is the end of our being,[6] the end of our performing a number of automatic functions that allowed us to maintain our balance in the face of a demanding and often threatening environment. Death is the end of the struggle to make things work, to keep them together, to show a consistency of plan and action, a directionality of will. Death is the end of responsibility, for what is no longer one can no longer be blamed.[7] And death is the end of time, of individual time at least, and the switching to an eternal instant where differences no longer hold, choices no longer need to be made, and before and after are no longer relevant.

Likewise, philosophy—triumphant, ideal philosophy—is perfect disinterest, complete liberation from utility, play for play's sake, loss of balance, acceptance and love of threats. Philosophy is unruliness, it is exploring both sides of the issue, it is defending a position and then destroying it, it is looking for hidden contradictions, it is wondering what you will, how you will, or that you will. Philosophy is before and beyond good and evil, it is the suspension of all moral constraints, it is the decision to call them in question, in a space within which they cannot (yet? ever?) legislate: "My reason is

---

[6] In *Letter* 2, pp. 1054–55, Montaigne says that La Boétie, as he approached death, had "nothing left but the likeness and shadow of a man, and [was], as he said about himself, *non homo, sed species hominis.*" At II 12, pp. 385–86, speaking to Plato "on behalf of human reason," he says: "[W]hen you say . . . that it will be for the spiritual part of man to enjoy the rewards of the other life, you tell us a thing of . . . little likelihood. . . . For by that reckoning, it will no longer be man, nor consequently ourselves, whom this enjoyment will concern; for we are built of two principal essential parts, whose separation is the death and destruction of our being." (This point, incidentally, is perfectly clear to Christians, who "know that divine justice embraces this association and union of body and soul, even to making the body capable of eternal rewards" [II 17, p. 485]).

[7] See I 7, p. 19: "Death, they say, acquits us of all our obligations."

not trained to bend and bow, it is my knees" (III 8, p. 714). And philosophy is rebellion against time, against the tyranny of time, against what needs to be done in an hour or a year; it is the freedom to use *all the time it takes* to follow an argument through its many intricate consequences, to explore innumerable perplexing objections, to test one story against all others, one voice against its echoes.

So it is not surprising that the scene that inaugurates philosophy,[8] the one where we first see philosophers at work, should also be the scene where the philosopher, for the first time, faces death. Philosophy *is* death: it is renouncing the day-to-day routine and jumping into the unknown, it is abolishing rules and breaking loose, and letting each of the many members of our internal pandemonium break loose as well. This is why the philosopher must not be afraid of death: not because he is a man, or an animal, or a living being, since fear of death might be very profitable for all these creatures as they struggle to survive, but *precisely because he is a philosopher*. To be afraid of death, for him, would be the same as forfeiting his task.

> [Julian the Apostate] owed to philosophy the singular contempt in which he held his life and all human things. (II 19, p. 508)

> Philosophy orders us to have death ever before our eyes. (III 12, p. 804)[9]

But *we* are not the child Socrates, and ours is not the ideal philosophical state. We do not belong in a happy limbo where time is no longer relevant and tales can be followed through. We have known the ways of the world, they have been imprinted in us as much as anybody, and will never let go. If only our knees are trained to bend, that is already bad enough: "reason" will have to fight long and hard against habit, and slowly and painfully try to *teach* the

---

[8] In more than a chronological sense, for remember: Socrates is philosophy's "tutor" (III 13, p. 855).

[9] The continuation of this passage is interesting, for there philosophy itself is said to "afterward [give] us the rules and precautions to provide against our being wounded by this foresight and this thought [of death]." See footnote 27 below.

knees not to bend. We can only "prepare" for death, and philosophy is only "apprenticeship and semblance" of it;[10] accepting and practicing death, that is, being truly and completely liberated, is another matter, a matter for beings of a different sort. "It belongs to the one and only Socrates to become acquainted with death with an ordinary countenance, to become familiar with it and play with it" (III 4, p. 632). For beings like ourselves, there is the constant struggle between the exigencies of life on the one hand—and the schooling that we received as a way to deal with them, and the respect that was bred in us for the moves taught by that schooling—and the gay wisdom of deviation and experiment on the other. There is only Pyrrho's way, who "*tried* [*essaya*], like all the others who were truly philosophers, to make his life correspond to his doctrine" (II 29, p. 533; italics mine). Which means that we will not be able to indulge in that wisdom and gaiety without shame, without experiencing the sense of a "sickness" that is wasting away precious energies and time.

"Premeditation of death is premeditation of freedom," Montaigne says, and "[h]e who has learned how to die has unlearned how to be a slave," because "[k]nowing how to die frees us from all subjection and constraint" (I 20, p. 60). Perhaps so, but such (un)learning is hard, and will not be over if (or when) we convince ourselves of the correctness of Montaigne's statements. That conviction will only be a beginning: the beginning of a long, difficult countertraining that one by one breaks all rules, contests all necessities, cuts all ties—all of this while rules, necessities, and ties *are still operational*; in particular, while they still kick and scream to maintain their grasp on us. While, that is, they make us feel deeply *wrong* for what we are doing.

So here you have it: the crime and the punishment. The crime is inevitable,[11] insofar as playing with fire is ultimately advantageous *and* this playing will happen inside (and by) agents who are still

---

[10] See also II 6, p. 267: "[A]s for death, we can try it only once: we are all apprentices when we come to it."

[11] More precisely, it is inevitable that behavior *conceptualized as* crime occurs. For additional motivation on this point, see the next section.

stuck to the old ways, and therefore must think of what they are doing as a fault.[12] And the punishment is inevitable, too. Doing philosophy is dying, all right, but for us it can only be dying a little,[13] and so long as we only die a little, so long as part of us is still alive and functioning, there will not only be longing for the absolute freedom death promises: there will also be fright over what that freedom means and implies.

Suicidal Attacks

But perhaps my description of the situation was too bleak, and unnecessarily so. True, the unlearning that philosophy consists of goes against the grain of tradition and the declared values of the community; but it still performs a function that is useful, and possibly vital, for that community, so why couldn't our declarations be different? Why couldn't we be up-front about the significance of this revolutionary enterprise and give the crazies a break: let them do their job in peace, without the obsession of being constitutionally at fault, of being intrinsically wrong? They won't be able to avoid the difficulty, the hardship, the loneliness connected with their task, but the guilt: why can't they live without that? They are doing it for us, aren't they? So why shouldn't they be aware of it, and happy, or at least proud, on account of it?

Montaigne says that "humility, fear, obedience, and amenability . . . are the principal qualities for the preservation of human society" (II 12, p. 368). And we can see the point of most of these traits: one needs to be humble with respect to authority, obedient to laws, and amenable to accord if the social machine based on that authority, those laws, and that accord is to work. But fear, what do we need it for? What is the point of this irrational sentiment—a senti-

---

[12] So these people will have to think that "[t]he curiosity to know things was given to men as a scourge" (II 17, p. 481; see also I 27, p. 135; III 5, p. 661).

[13] See III 4, p. 634: "I love to see these leading souls unable to shake off our common lot. Perfect men as they are, [philosophers] still . . . are men, and most heavily so."

ment that, we know already, Montaigne *fears* more than anything else?[14] Couldn't we be more detached about the whole matter: recognize the advantages of humble, obedient, and amenable behavior without being shaken and torn inside by something as uncontrollable, urgent, and blind as fear?[15]

Sometimes, fear does not work. It is no use to be afraid of conspirators, for example, "witness so many Roman emperors. A man who finds himself in this danger should not expect much from his strength or his vigilance" (I 24, p. 94). The reason for such hopelessness is an instructive one: "whoever holds his own life in scorn will always be master of that of others" (ibid.). That is, some people simply will not be blackmailed, they will laugh at the "vengeance and punishment" (ibid.) you throw at them, and consequently there will be no way to keep them in line.

> [I]t is a dangerous obligation and a handicap to keep yourself in check and within the rules, in all matters and places, against those who are free as air, to whom everything is permissible that can advance their plan, who have neither law nor order except to follow their advantage. (I 23, p. 89)

True revolutionaries—those who do not simply imagine new worlds, but try to bring them about—are people of this kind: they hold their life in scorn and thus give you no chance, no bargaining power, no room for maneuver. Either you succeed in enforcing power, physical power, on them or you are lost—and constantly enforcing power on all of them is more than anybody can do, at some crucial junctures of history. It would be more than anybody can ever do if fear did not work inside (many of) them, too, and turn them into fainthearted, half-baked, vociferous clowns. Your

---

[14] See p. 53 above. Note that an interesting pragmatic paradox results from fearing fear, since this attitude (as opposed, for example, to despising or ridiculing fear) involves *experiencing* the very fear you fear, and hence essentially admitting its inevitability at the very time you take a negative stand on it.

[15] See I 47, p. 208: "[T]here is no passion so contagious as that of fear, nor so easily caught on faith, nor quicker to spread."

fear can only be effective if it mirrors itself in mine; if mine goes, yours becomes a useless impediment, and you and I may be lost.

But let us go slower, since the goal is an important one and the terrain is slippery. What we are considering is the following suggestion: since the philosopher's task is as important to the community as the cobbler's or the judge's, the philosopher need not make too much of the apparent individualism that colors his activity, and need not be bothered by the moral scruples that tend to attach themselves to individualisms of all sorts. He only *seems* to go against the crowd; in fact, he *and* the crowd are going to be better in the end because of the ways he explores and the absurdities he takes seriously. By educating himself to face death, he is promoting everybody's longer and happier life, so he should proceed to thus educate himself in all serenity, without internal turmoil, without self-accusation, without shame. Indeed, eliminating guilt and reproach from his horizon might make him able to do his work better, to approach the end of his education sooner, to become more and more like the gay, blasphemous child that constitutes his elusive ideal. Who knows? Maybe this ill-conceived guilt is the only reason why the ideal is elusive.

The problem with this suggestion is that, unless properly checked, the game of philosophy is too dangerous, in the precise sense that it gives its players too much power over all of us—the power of those who hold their life in scorn, of those who are not afraid to "speak to the magistrate . . . with an irreverent and uncivil liberty" (I 25, p. 98).[16] Which is not to say that the power will necessarily be misused, but it is to say that nobody can afford the risk, since "[the philosophers'] instruction, . . . if it does not work for good, works for evil" (ibid., p. 104), and "the extremity of philosophy is harmful, and . . . makes a man wild and vicious, disdainful of common religions and laws, an enemy of social intercourse, an enemy of human pleasures, incapable of any political administration and of helping either others or himself, fit to be slapped with im-

---

[16] See also II 17, p. 498: "Obedience is not pure or tranquil in a man who reasons and argues."

punity" (I 30, p. 146). To be crystal clear about it, we cannot afford the risk of letting loose a group of kamikazes, who, because they are not afraid of death and perhaps even love it, will not be restrained within the bounds that circumscribe everybody else's activity, and, because they play with loss of balance all the time, will constantly threaten to unbalance the social and political structure. We need to set our agents on their tracks, the agents of dissuasion and distrust; we need to make them turn against, torture, and ruin themselves, not to the point of making them totally ineffective in their role as guinea pigs, but enough for their irresponsible play not to spread outside the lab. Their fear of void, their penitence, and their anguish are not just an unfortunate, temporary outcome of the conflict unlearning has staged inside them with learning (or having learned): it is an opportune precaution to make it impossible, or at least unlikely, that the world as we know it will come to an abrupt end. And Nature, or whatever agency is responsible for all this business of adaptation, is cautious indeed, so much so that, in general, what is opportune will also happen.

A large part of the *Essays* is constituted by a reflection on the great protagonists of human history, and on what made them great. Alexander, Caesar, and Epaminondas are as familiar to these pages as Socrates, and far more than any other "professional philosopher."[17] One might ask, why? Because such men, not any scholars or bookworms, are the ultimate examples of defiance of death, the supreme explorers of what, for others, are unthinkable options, the true worshippers of imagination, the "great and illustrious souls" for whom only "it is tolerable . . . to take unusual liberties" (I 26, p. 114),[18] those who did not content themselves with saying, as Montaigne does, "It is pricing our life exactly as it really is to abandon it

[17] At I 20, p. 58, Alexander is said to be "[t]he greatest man that was simply a man" (and is compared with Jesus Christ). At III 12, p. 793, Socrates is said to be "the man most worthy to be known and to be presented to the world as an example."

[18] At II 36, p. 571, Montaigne says, concerning men like Alexander, that "it is impossible to conduct such great movements according to the rules of justice," and that they "require to be judged in gross, by the master purpose of their actions." And at I 14, p. 46, he says that "[t]o judge of great and lofty things we need a soul of the same caliber."

for a dream" (III 4, p. 638), but accepted the challenge of living by that statement. They are, in a way, philosophy come to earth: not the shaky, trembling philosophy of those who are afraid to try, but philosophy in all of its actuality and impudence, bold philosophy, scandalous philosophy, the philosophy that has made provocation into a business. Their pride, their ambition, their patriotism, or simply their courage are not "double within themselves," carry no afterthoughts, but proceed straight like an arrow as they drift through nations and armies and continents following their own private vision, ruthless and indifferent to what the vision costs. They are the true, the innocent children, those who do play for play's sake, and enjoy it. It is thinking of them, and speaking in the name of all of us scared and tormented characters, that Montaigne says: "If my mind could gain a firm footing, I would not make essays, I would make decisions" (III 2, p. 611).[19] And it is with the intimate regret of the ineffectual hairsplitter that he evokes Caesar's inexorable verdict: "[A] man must carry out, not deliberate about, high enterprises" (II 34, p. 560).

But each of those men brought misfortune, at best on himself, at worst on his city or country.[20] In the luckiest circumstances, *they* were exiled or killed; otherwise, it was the community itself that suffered demise, or a tyranny worse than death. Again, this may be a coincidence, and things might go differently; but remember, Montaigne's concern is with what *can* happen, and the fact that this destruction can happen is bad enough. We must make sure that it won't happen, we must minimize the chances that shameless mutants such as those mentioned become part of our landscape. And in order to do this, two suggestions are in order.

[19] See also III 9, p. 759: "One man . . . produces Essays, who cannot produce results." Even concerning more modest, personal health matters, Montaigne complains: "I am sorry I did not have the boldness, as I had the desire, and with some reason, to drink in the bath in the morning" (*Travel Journal*, p. 1001).

[20] At II 33, p. 554, Montaigne says that Caesar "made his memory abominable to all good men, because he willed to seek his glory in the ruin of his country and the subversion of the most powerful and flourishing republic that the world will ever see."

First, revolution must not be made accessible to everyone.[21] Paradoxically, but consistently with the argument developed so far, it is only after a long period of training in the traditional ways, and after making sure that one's soul is steady enough—that is, that it will offer resistance to, and suffer from, unlearning—that it becomes safe to expose one to the risks of doubting and challenging ordinary beliefs. Speaking of religious knowledge, Montaigne says:

> It is not everyone's study; it is the study of the persons who are dedicated to it. . . . The wicked, the ignorant, grow worse by it. . . . Comical folk, those who think they have made it fit for the people to handle because they have put it into the language of the people! . . . Pure ignorance that relied entirely on others was much more salutary, and more learned, than this vain and verbal knowledge, the nurse of presumption and temerity. (I 56, p. 232)

As for learning in general, and philosophical learning in particular, it "is a thing of great weight," which is why "so many inept souls . . . collapse under it" (III 8, p. 711). "They would have made good husbandmen, good tradesmen, good artisans," and they end up instead "corrupt[ing] the dignity of philosophy in handling it" (ibid.). Beware of them: of those weak minds that are ready to catch the fire they play with and spread it, the potential Alexanders and Caesars of this world, or their (tragic) caricatures. "What shall we say of the fact that even doubt and inquiry strikes our imagination and changes us? Those who yield suddenly to these propensities bring total ruin upon themselves" (III 13, p. 831).

Finally, speaking of instruction, in particular of the instruction *he* can provide, Montaigne says that his nature "is unsuited, either in speaking or in writing, for beginners," and that consequently he greatly dislikes "to go and preach at the first passer-by and play schoolmasters to the ignorance or ineptitude of the first man we meet" (III 8, p. 716). So much for the first word of caution: don't

---

[21] Note how what is forthcoming here is "more of an answer" to the question considered on p. 40.

preach the gospel of philosophy too widely and inconsiderately, or you will be cutting your own (and everybody else's) throat. As for the second word, well, that is a longer story.

The Philosopher's Cave

"I am of the opinion," Montaigne says, "that the most honorable occupation is to serve the public and to be useful to many" (III 9, p. 727). This is not surprising: if the highest ideal is for the community to survive and prosper, each of us must be ready to bring his little, precious contribution to social welfare, and "benefit some neighbor" by the "fruits of [his] genius, virtue, and all excellence" (ibid.; quoted from Cicero). The man Montaigne, however, prefers to "stay out of it," and wishes "to find a son-in-law who could spoon-feed [his] old age comfortably and put it to sleep" (ibid.). The dire necessities of public life are too much for him, and he wants out: "The public welfare requires that a man betray and lie and massacre; let us resign this commission to more obedient and suppler [*plus souples*] people" (III 1, p. 600).

Following this inclination, Montaigne studiously avoided social commitments, shunned the court, and kept his distance from the religious and political Armageddon of which the France of those years was the unfortunate theater. Also (and most important), when he did hold a public position of some significance—that of mayor of Bordeaux—he showed in it none of the "suppleness" that was such a distinctive feature of his private games, and that he appropriately attributes to dedicated public people in the last passage above. He was a conscientious, balanced, conservative officer, we know:[22] one who withdrew without residue into the safe, sensible management of the existing state of affairs. "We must live in the world and make the most of it such as we find it," he says in this connection (III 10, p. 774), and probably because he feels such conventional behavior like an external imposition, like something with which he

---

[22] See footnotes 3 and 4 of Chapter 3 and the attending text.

cannot identify, he makes it clear that "[t]he mayor and Montaigne
have always been two, with a clear separation" (ibid.).

There is a good reason for Montaigne's passivity and tendential
"laziness" with respect to social commitments: they are directly antagonistic to the intellectual activities where he has chosen to direct
most of his energies. Either you imagine other worlds or you ad-
minister this one; both you cannot do, at least not at the same time.
And he offers all sorts of excuses for his attitude, too: he has "little
qualification" for "such employments," and has seen people so
much better than himself nevertheless abstain from them.[23] But
now we are in a position to see deeper than that reason or these
excuses: we can see that it was not just personal inclination or modesty that made Montaigne avoid publicity, or stay put when he had
to accept it. An important *political* problem is at stake here—the
very problem we discussed in the preceding section.

How shall we tend to the seeds of change and revolution, in order
to have them ready when they might be of use, while at the same
time preventing them from growing too fast and too wide, and
compromising that stability which is to be defended at all costs,
even at the cost of revolution when nothing else works, but only
then? We have one answer already: block their spread, make it a
condition of planting them that the ground be solid and firm, and
that a solid and firm vegetation of a more conventional nature sur-
rounds them and fights with them for the limited resources of air
and light. A second answer is forthcoming now: make it all happen,
as much as possible, in an artificial environment—a greenhouse, not
a forest—an environment cut off from connections with the natural
world. Let it be a closed system, a black box, a miniature copy of
the real thing perhaps, but a copy whose ties with the real thing have
been severed, since each of those ties is a possible vehicle of infection, a route for the viruses to take as they make their way into the
social structure and spread terror there.[24] Let philosophers be not

[23] See III 9, p. 727.
[24] At III 8, p. 704, we are told that "it is impossible to say how much [our mind]
loses and degenerates by our continual association and frequentation with mean and
sickly minds," since "[t]here is no contagion that spreads like that one," and at III 12,

only limited in number, and tormented by guilt, but also isolated, imprisoned in their ghettos, and pragmatically inefficient.[25] Let them follow Montaigne's example and "stay out of it."

Throughout this book, my characterization of philosophy has been increasingly deviant and worrisome. Philosophy is transgression, philosophy is play, philosophy is death. But no suggestion is more deviant, and less welcome for the philosopher's self-image, than the political recipe of the preceding paragraph. Since there was philosophy, its practitioners have depicted themselves as the wise, who have a right and duty to enlighten others. The itinerary that brought them enlightenment may have been long and tortuous, and chance, fate, or supernatural powers may have played a decisive role in it. Perhaps they fell and were hit on their way to Damascus, perhaps they were born with the memories of past lives, perhaps predestination chose them for its obscure ends, or perhaps they were just smarter, more resourceful, and more dedicated than their peers, and were looking in the right direction, where the Forms shone. But whatever the reason, at some point they have seen the truth. Before that happened, it was proper to laugh at them: there is nothing more ridiculous than the devilish, groundless pride of those who try the out-of-the-way paths and end up running in circles and getting lost. After it happened, however, those for whom it happened had to go back into the cave and tell the prisoners there what it was really like, what those shadows on the walls really stood for, where the light came from. And at that time, the prisoners had to follow them, for what better chance of liberation did they have than the advice of those who had been out and seen it all?

And since the beginning, there have been occasional suggestions that this picture was a fake. They came from the outsiders, from those whom the professionals were quick to dismiss as not being really philosophers, but intellectual anarchists, cheap literati, Sun-

---

p. 794, that "[t]here is . . . some [learning] which, under color of curing us, poisons us."

[25] See II 12, p. 366: "What is all that but philosophy confessing her impotence, and sending us back not merely to ignorance, to be under cover, but to stupidity itself, to insensibility and nonexistence?"

day preachers, jacks-of-all-trades. Such humbugs insinuated that there was no truth to be found, or at least not to be found in books, that the stories written there satisfied some other drive, and that it was dangerous to take them too seriously. And possibly those making such insinuations were in fact anarchists and preachers and humbugs, and they had, consciously or unconsciously, less than noble aims in making their insinuations, but the fact of the matter is: we have now come to agree with them, in terms of substance if not of detail.

The key to the agreement is a fundamental reversal in the relation between theory and practice, promoted by Montaigne's *Essays* and rehearsed in the present work.[26] According to the traditional view of this relation, one first gets the true theory, the correct representation of reality, and then on the basis of that theory comes up with practices that are successful *because* (and insofar as) the theory is true. According to the view that has emerged here, on the other hand, what comes conceptually first is the correctness of a practice, which reduces to its being entrenched in a community and its contributing to the integration of that community within its environment. The issue of relating this practice to a theory arises when we feel the necessity to justify the practice,[27] and we feel that necessity when we begin to throw the practice into the open field of all possible alternative practices, and we begin to worry about such alternatives when we begin to experiment with contrary-to-fact situations, when we give free rein to imagination. Thus theorizing (for Montaigne, philosophizing) is but one of the practices, a very useful one and quite likely the most human of all, but one that has in the end only pragmatic significance and promises no special insight or wisdom: "Wonder is the foundation of all philosophy, inquiry its

[26] A good summary of Montaigne's attitude in this regard (for which Chapter 2 above is especially relevant) can be found at III 5, pp. 639–40: "My philosophy is in action, in natural and present practice, little in fancy." See also my "Theories and Practices."

[27] This justification is usually realized through a "rationalizing" use of the same (potentially deconstructing) activity of storytelling that created the problem in the first place (as with doctors and lawyers; see footnote 4 of Chapter 5 and the attending text). See also footnotes 9 and 10 of Chapter 7 and the attending text.

progress, ignorance its end" (III 11, p. 788). If anything, it promises blood and tears, and requires handling with special care. It requires that its performers be made prisoners, that *they* be locked in a cave, and that there be as little contact as possible between the shadows *they* look at—those fantastic, "abstract" ghosts of theirs devoid of all life—and the real bodies ordinary people deal with. They who are the freest to experiment must also be the most impotent to act,[28] and others will be best advised not to heed them, not to try to understand them, not to follow their lead. They fall in wells, you know, they have their heads in the clouds.

Occasionally, these words are taken literally, and philosophers are thrown into physical jails, or worse. But most often, this extreme measure is not necessary. Philosophers have their own ways of making themselves isolated and useless, they have their own special kinds of caves. One of these has already implicitly surfaced in our discourse, so it will only be a matter of bringing it to a clear statement. Ironically, and not a bit perversely, but for reasons that by now give it a ring of inevitability, this discipline whose point is restless challenge and revolution has been reified, sedimented, and conglutinated into an institution. Laws (of reason) have been promulgated to shape its (ideal) community, a jargon—incomprehensible to most—has been erected as a barrier against relevance, and a specific problem-area as much as possible remote from all impact on other practices has been designated as the pasture for the bona fide members of the clan. Several independent motivations, all cited earlier, have acted in determining this reality:[29] the necessity of slowly detaching oneself from the inflexible logic of everyday concerns if one wants to have a chance of attacking that logic and articulating alternatives to it, the necessity of discouraging the majority from meddling with such detachment and attacks, and now the necessity

[28] There is an interesting analogy between this situation and that of dreams, where (as noted, for example, by Freud) we can give expression to our wildest desires only because our motor apparatus is paralyzed.

[29] At III 9, p. 733, Montaigne says of the Roman state: "The fabric of so great a body holds together by more than a single nail. It holds together even by its antiquity, like old buildings whose foundations have been worn away by age, without cement or mortar, which yet live and support themselves by their own weight."

of making those who went through the detachment into ineffective Cassandras, whose concerns nobody cares about. Carried by the strength of so many independent grounds, philosophy as an institution has become a formidable machine, capable of surviving and using precious resources in the middle of the direst necessities, resistant to the fall of kings and the demise of peoples, stubbornly attached to its own tradition and values. Within this solid, thick, indestructible body, experimentation and play can continue with minimal risk, since those inside and those outside it, more often than not, will look at each other with the same snobbish contemptuousness,[30] and proceed as if the other did not exist. Furthermore, if this trick were not enough, there is a second one, with which the first is ordinarily combined, and to which we must now turn our attention.

[30] At I 25, p. 98, we are reminded that "philosophers, who are remote from all public occupation, . . . have also in truth sometimes been mocked by the comic license of their times, their opinions and ways making them ridiculous," and that "the common herd disdained them as ignorant of the elementary and common things, as presumptuous and insolent." Given Montaigne's somewhat schizophrenic personality, it is not surprising that he should have a similar attitude with respect to *his own* wisdom and judgment. Thus in *Travel Journal*, pp. 999–1000, he says: "[T]oday certain doctors who had to hold an important consultation for a young lord . . . came to ask me, at his behest, to be good enough to hear their opinions and arguments, because he was resolved to rely wholly on my judgment. I laughed about this to myself."

CHAPTER SEVEN

THE BOOK

To this child, such as it is, what I give I give purely and
irrevocably, as one gives to the children of one's body.
The little good I have done for it is no longer at my
disposal. . . . If I am wiser than it, it is richer than I.

(II 8, p. 293)

෪

By Words Alone

WE KNOW already from Chapter 4 that Montaigne's "dreams" are
verbal, linguistic, written ones; we know that it is in the medium of
language that he conducts the experiments suggested by his imagination. We will see now that this is not a peculiarity of his: language, for good reasons, is for most people the primary outlet of
revolutionary drives.

In the last of the *Essays,* Montaigne gives a spirited description of
the "natural infirmity of [human] mind," of how "it does nothing
but ferret and quest, and keeps incessantly whirling around, building up and becoming entangled in its own work, . . . and is suffocated in it" (III 13, p. 817). Giving up this quest is, for the mind, to
give up its own nature: a mind that stops and rests, content with
what it has found, is simply less of a mind, "it is only half alive"
(ibid., p. 818). Imaginary lights and truths glimmer in the distance,
and make the mind start in its restless pursuit, but then the pursuit
becomes an end in itself:[1] it becomes "boundless and without form

---

[1] See II 12, p. 379 ("The very search for great and occult things is very pleasant,
even to him who gains from it nothing but reverence and fear of judging them"); III

. . . an irregular, perpetual motion, without model and without aim" (ibid.).

I have already indicated the rationale of this crazy (?) wandering: "The world is but a perennial movement. . . . Stability itself is nothing but a more languid motion" (III 2, p. 610). Therefore, we must keep our options open and continue to search, not because there is necessarily anything to find but because the searching process itself is of value: it trains us for what is not there but could be there, and if it is, so much the better for those who already know how to dance. This much is not new; what deserves attention here is the particular form the wandering takes.

As a result of the explosive creativity contemplated above, some might expect a world bursting with invention and transgression: a world where people are constantly stepping over boundaries and looking for the Indies and blowing out the tyrant's brains. But this is not the way Montaigne sees it: what the world is doing instead is "swarming with commentaries" (III 13, p. 818). The main occupation of boundless, irresistible mind is writing books about books about books, interpreting the interpretations much more than interpreting the things, getting farther and farther away from nonverbal reality, up a ladder of opinions "grafted upon one another" (ibid.): "The world is nothing but babble, and I never saw a man who did not say rather more than less than he should" (I 26, p. 124).

The ideology of this interpretive task is, of course, one of detecting the hidden meanings of the authors. But like the truths glimmering in the distance, these meanings are bound to reveal themselves as delusive, imaginary foci. "The hundredth commentator hands [the book] on to his successor thornier and rougher than the first one had found it" (III 13, p. 817), an outcome which is only to be expected because all we do, and can do, is "exchange one word for another word, often more unknown" (ibid., p. 819), and by mobilizing all these words we do nothing but "obscure and bury the meaning" (ibid., p. 817). Or perhaps we effectively counteract, in

---

13, p. 854 ("The fruit and goal of their pursuit is to pursue, as Alexander said that the purpose of his work was to work").

practice if not in theory, the *concept* of meaning as a unique entity canonically associated with an utterance or inscription, and show the quest for meaning for what it is: a process whereby a reader projects onto a text his interests, his needs, his desires, and ends up forcing the text in directions that the author could not even be aware of. "Speech belongs half to the speaker, half to the listener," Montaigne says (ibid., p. 834), and as for the written word, "[a]n able reader often discovers in other men's writings perfections beyond those that the author put in or perceived, and lends them richer meanings and aspects" (I 24, p. 93).[2]

Thus reading and interpretation, often depicted as what brings order and harmony to our relation with the Other, turn out to be the principal theater of that cultural drift which is such an essential part of culture itself: the stage of deviation and variation, of experiment for experiment's sake. And so it is with language, the fundamental tool mobilized on this stage: "In view of the continual variation that has prevailed in [our language] up to now, who can hope that its present form will be in use fifty years from now? It slips out of our hands every day, and has halfway changed since I have been alive" (III 9, p. 751).

We have already seen that Montaigne uses books "not so much for instruction as for exercise";[3] now we can be told that in general "great authors . . . speak truly and usefully enough if they speak ingeniously" (III 6, p. 685), and that ideas "are true and sound enough if they are useful and pleasing" (III 9, p. 726). And by the same token, endless interpretation is also a major arena for fighting, for that iconoclastic aggressiveness that usually does *not* find expression in direct revolutionary action. "[A]nimosity and bitterness" surface "in commenting [no less] than in inventing" (III 13, p. 815), and in fact, "in the liberal arts there are several subjects whose essence is controversy and dispute, and which have no life apart from that," producing as they do "great, lengthy altercations . . . fit only for the exercise [!] of our minds" (III 9, p. 730).

---

[2] See also I 11, p. 29; I 26, p. 115; II 12, p. 442; III 8, p. 710. This theme is discussed in my "A New Paradigm of Meaning."

[3] See p. 73 above.

A more conventional view of the matter than the one I have been exploring and endorsing here might find these statements quite acceptable. In such a view, the mind's objective is not—not directly at least—concrete, physical reality, but rather ideas or representations, and possibly words or phrases that signify those "mental contents." So if the mind is regarded as the agent of renovation and change, one must expect that this change and renovation take place primarily in the airy, "abstract" locus of objects *of thought* and *of discourse* and only later *possibly* extend, by a practical application that does not in any case touch their (ideal) "essence," to those other (?) objects that impinge upon our sensory apparatus.[4] But for us here, this easy justification won't do: "the mind" has been characterized already as the more erratic and restless component of our practices, "the body" as the more blindly traditional, and "the abstraction" generating the realm of the mental as the straining of practices outside their contexts, the bottomless pursuing of the contrary-to-fact, the bold confronting those other moves that, for reasons unfathomable as they are awesome, *are simply not made*. As a result of the continuity thus established, we may have less of a problem in bringing together "mind" and "body," but right now our explanation of the affinity between revolution and language must be different from what is offered by the two-world doctrine of the conventional view. There are no two worlds: there is only one, in which some things are done according to custom and some are done in new, unsettling ways. As it turns out, most of the latter things happen by words alone, and only rarely do such words spread into "real" actions—those actions, that is, that people perform "with their arm" rather than "with their tongue" (*Letter* 8, p. 1064). But why? Why tongues more than arms? Why is "discussion" the "most fruitful and natural exercise of our mind" (III 8, p. 704)?

At this stage of the game, answers to these questions are relatively easy, and not only that: through these answers, we can do more than explain the affinity between revolution and language. We can begin

---

[4] The question of whether "real" objects are to be identified with some of the intentional ones need not be addressed here. For some discussion of it, see my *Kant's Copernican Revolution*.

to explain—not simply hypostatize by means of the two-world doctrine mentioned above—the affinity between language *and mind*: why mind, that is, being the revolutionary agency it is, *should* have language as its main operational tool and verbal residues—or thoughts[5]—as the *differentia* marking its essence and specificity.

A Vile and Vulgar Merchandise

In 1568 Montaigne finished his translation of Raymond Sebond's *Theologia Naturalis* and dedicated it to his father, who had originally commissioned it. The dedication contains the following words:

> [I]n exchange for his excellent and very religious arguments, his lofty and as it were divine conceptions, it will turn out that you for your part have brought to him only words and language: a merchandise so vulgar and so vile that the more of it a man has, the less, peradventure, he is worth. (*Letter* 3, p. 1056)

Montaigne's contempt for language and for what can only be expressed in language, that is, learning, is commonplace in the *Essays*. It is no wonder, he says, "that our ancestors took no great account of letters, . . . [since] they teach us neither to think well nor to do well" (I 25, p. 103). All there is to "jurisprudence, medicine, teaching, and even theology" nowadays is "the aim of getting rich by them": if it weren't for this disreputable desire, "you would undoubtedly see them in as wretched condition as they ever were"

---

[5] That thoughts *can* be conceived as nothing but unspoken words, and the practice of thinking them nothing but the "abstraction" of telling a story without a public—hence not as the manifestation of a distinct, and more dignified, reality—has been suggested all along in this book: specifically, at least whenever I tried to establish a continuity between "mind" and "body." (An additional suggestion to this effect comes from II 12, p. 391, where Montaigne conjectures that men without mouths might have no reason either.) In the next chapter, I will bring forth an argument for why some such words *should* be unspoken, that is, for why there should be thoughts (thus conceived) at all. (This promissory note justifies the "begin to" qualification given in the text above.)

(ibid.).[6] We know from Chapter 2 some of the reasons for this negative judgment. Verbal communication and learning do not help us cope with the environment, are not conducive to that "practical memory" by which we situate and adjust ourselves there; in fact they can even be counterproductive if our end is adaptation. But this cannot be the whole story, for it does not explain the fascination that is induced by learning—and that must be admitted at the very moment in which we complain that some try to cash in on it. It does not explain why, in spite of so much uselessness and counterproductiveness, people have forever been indulging in words and "letters." It does not explain why Montaigne himself, after discounting most "subtleties" as "nothing but verbal quibbles," should "not want to expose them any further" inasmuch as they "may be done usefully" (III 12, p. 795). So there is a use to quibbles after all? And what is it?

In the dedication quoted above, Montaigne does not just say that language is vile and vulgar: he also says that it is a vile and vulgar *merchandise*. The word "merchandise" reminds one of the market, and the market is a place where some things are exchanged for others. A vile *thing* is a lowly, detestable one, but a vile merchandise is something more specific: something that is not worth its price, that is inadvertently, perhaps dishonestly, exchanged for a more valuable item, that leaves us disappointed, in need of a refund.[7] Let us pursue this metaphor a little further and see what, if anything, we can learn from it.

Often we get words, empty, elusive words, in exchange for things. We might indeed like to search for the Indies or blow the tyrant's brains out, we might like to exercise our curiosity by get-

---

[6] See also II 12, p. 426: "You recite a case simply to a lawyer, he answers you wavering and doubtful, you feel that it is a matter of indifference to him whether he undertakes to support one party or the other. Have you paid him well . . . ? . . . Behold an evident and indubitable truth that appears to his intelligence. He discovers a wholly new light on your case, and believes it in all conscience."

[7] It is interesting to note that Montaigne strongly dislikes the situation of the market, to the point of accepting a loss to get out of it. At I 14, p. 43, he says: "There is nothing I hate like bargaining. It is a pure interchange of trickery and shamelessness. . . . And so I used to borrow at a disadvantage."

ting lost in the forest and finding our way again, to explore counterfactual possibilities *in concreto* by pursuing a glance, a smile, a gesture to its ultimate consequences, and what we do *instead* is talk:
petulant, insignificant babble. We add word upon word and thus
pacify ourselves; we tell stories rather than live them and thus find
a stupid, substitutive satisfaction.[8] We conjure the echoes of experiences that will always remain unreal, and we content ourselves
with exploring all nuances of those echoes, as if they were the real
thing. And we are happy if the nuances are intricate, if they keep us
busy, for what shall we do with our time otherwise? What would
retirement be, without crossword puzzles?

> Why did not only Aristotle but most philosophers affect dif-
> ficulty, if not to bring out the vanity of the subject, and keep
> the curiosity of our mind amused by giving it fodder in gnaw-
> ing on this hollow and fleshless bone? . . . Difficulty is a *coin*
> that the learned employ, like conjurors, in order not to reveal
> the vanity of their art, and which human stupidity readily ac-
> cepts as *payment*. . . . (II 12, p. 376; italics mine)

Payment indeed: a vile, vulgar, bony currency in exchange for the
flesh and blood of the life we did not live, of the Indies we did not
reach.

But consider: *could* we—would it be reasonable—to send everybody who's interested on the Indies' tracks? Could we allow all potential revolutionaries to become actual tyrannicides? We already
know that the answer is no. The point of revolution is what *can*
happen, so we must make sure that until it *does* happen this restless
fooling around does not interfere with the blind repetitiveness that
is our best guarantee of efficient performance. To make interference

---

[8] See II 16, p. 477: "Since men, because of their inadequacy, cannot be sufficiently
paid with good money, let false be employed too." Also, more specifically, "as
women wear ivory teeth where their natural ones are lacking, and in place of their
real complexion fabricate one of some foreign matter . . . so does science. . . . She
gives us in *payment* and as presuppositions the things that she herself teaches us are
invented. . . . As also, for that matter, philosophy offers us not what is, or what it
believes, but the most plausible and pleasant thing it *forges*" (II 12, p. 401; italics
mine).

impossible, on the other hand, we need to make *contact* impossible, and how better can we achieve this end than by giving the crazies an "abstract"—that is, separate, divided—turf on which to do their exercise, a bodiless medium where they can stage all their presumptuous uselessness? "Dionysius used to make fun of the grammarians who are at pains to inquire about the troubles of Ulysses and are ignorant of their own; the musicians who attune their flutes and do not attune their morals; the orators who study to talk justice, not to do it" (I 25, p. 101).

Give the intellectuals words to play with: things we will keep for ourselves, and we will let them believe that words open up to them a reality much more elevated and dignified than this sublunar planet of ours, a reality of which all that is under the moon is but a pale reflection. If that's what it takes for them to do their work, so be it. We shall give them the respect they demand, and laugh at their stupidity when they are not looking. If need be—that is, if they become too involved and meddlesome, if they insist too earnestly on a practical application of their nonsense—we can always use their own weapons against themselves: stories that rationalize our existing practices against those that would challenge them, stories that depict this "world" as the best of all against those that made us think of *other* worlds—and hence of this *as a world*—in the first place. See how many things "[m]y mind," which "has no lack of plausible reasons for all things," can find to "relieve [my imagination] . . . of all trouble and conflict" (III 13, p. 836):

> It tells me that it is for my own good that I have the stone; that buildings of my age must naturally suffer some leakage. . . . That the company should console me, since I have fallen into the commonest ailment of men of my time of life. . . . That of the men who are stricken by it there are few that get off more cheaply. . . .
>
> "Fear of this disease," says my mind, "used to terrify you, when it was unknown to you. . . . It is an affliction that punishes those of your members by which you have most sinned. . . .

"The fear and pity that people feel for this illness is a subject of vainglory for you." (Ibid.)[9]

And see how powerful our inventions can be to disarm those of our opponents, and how useful that is when the latter have revolutionary aims.

> And even if we strip [Sebond's arguments] of this ornament and of the help and approbation of faith, and take them as purely human fancies, to combat those who are precipitated into the frightful and horrible darkness of irreligion, they will still be found as solid and as firm as any others of the same type that may be opposed to them; so that we shall be in a position to say to our adversaries—'If you have better, bring it out; if not, give in' (Horace). (II 12, p. 327)[10]

We know that all these stories are useless anyway, and may well remain useless even if the premises on which they are built were to become true: when words are separated from things, and left hanging in the air, there is no guarantee that they *say* anything.[11] But then, we cannot ask for any such guarantee, all we are asking for is an extra chance, one more than the dinosaurs had. This extra chance the intellectuals do provide, and our community is affluent enough, and lazy enough, to afford the luxury of their presence.

So far, so good, then. We can have our cake and eat it, too. We can encourage the respect of tradition—in fact, we can punish any rule-breaking—and at the same time cultivate the germs of future,

[9] Note, however, that this connection can work both ways. Not only does mind protect us from imagination (and hence from itself), but the stories it uses for that purpose may ultimately increase the imagination's impact: "What if knowledge, trying to arm us with new defenses against natural mishaps, has imprinted in our fancy their magnitude and weight, more than her reasons and subtleties to protect us from them?" (III 12, p. 795) More details about this defensive use of stories—defensive, that is, of actual practices—can be found in my *Kant's Copernican Revolution* and "Philosophy One and Two."

[10] See also ibid., p. 328; ibid., p. 372; II 37, p. 589. Incidentally, the practice of opposing one "story" to another, thereby showing the weakness of both, was typical of Pyrrho, one of those "ancients" that had the most influence on Montaigne.

[11] This is, in the last analysis, the problem of "real" versus logical possibility, which is a central one in *Kant's Copernican Revolution*.

different traditions in a linguistic greenhouse where all graftings can
be tried, all monstrosities patiently nurtured, thus insulating ourselves from the infection that those monstrosities might produce
while hedging our bets as to how stable the world is going to be.
We can play with "the empty husks that peel off from the things,"
with the "filmy shells" that "the cicadas leave behind," while
"scarcely look[ing] at things in gross and alone" (III 4, p. 635). We
can, can't we?

Well, ask the gardeners. Think of what *they* are getting in exchange for life in the greenhouse. The vile merchandise of inconclu-
sive rambling, the empty promise that their efforts might have
some unspecified use, the stale gaiety of old boys' reunions, the
guilt of always having to try too far, too deep, too much. How
would you like that? Wonder why Montaigne doesn't?

> Here you have . . . some excrements of an aged mind, now
> hard, now loose, and always undigested. And when shall I
> make an end of describing the continual agitation and changes
> of my thoughts, whatever subject they light on, since Didy-
> mus filled six thousand books with the sole subject of gram-
> mar? What must prattle produce, when the stammering and
> loosening of the tongue smothered the world with such a hor-
> rible load of volumes? So many words for the sake of words
> alone! O Pythagoras, why did you not conjure away this tem-
> pest? (III 9, p. 721)

The Way to Babel

But now forget about the philosopher's lack of self-esteem and
other psychological troubles, and concentrate on how he is to perform his task. A major difficulty here is the following: if revolution
is mostly confined to language, language is not at all confined to
talk of revolutionary endeavors. It is not just the learned that voice
echoes, it is not just the dreamers that spell out their fantasies aloud:
there are also family men and women telling their children how to

behave, anchormen displaying the news, and politicians regurgitat-
ing the olds. None of the latter classes of people has (alas!) anything
much to say that is deviant or exciting, but still they do speak, they
use language as much as anybody, and they use it in ways that are
as traditional, codified, and rigorous as any practice will ever be. In
fact, very few activities are as explicitly regulated by a *grammar* as
speaking and writing, and for no other activity is this grammar so
widely circulated and imposed throughout society. Is it still possible, in the face of so much conformism, to use language as a
means—indeed, as the primary means—of renovation and violence?

The answer to this question must be a negative one, unless and
until violence is brought to bear upon language itself. The social
network of practices and values has a way of defending itself—automatically and unreflectively—against all potential sources of un-
rest. So even with this remote and relatively harmless, "theoretical"
flirting with the unknown, there is no hope of being left alone to
play with it, in a place where tensions are forever relieved and
dreams aren't forgotten. A war will have to be fought here, too: not
an explosive catharsis that once and for all destroys all structure and
maximizes randomness, but an exhausting, interminable guerrilla
skirmish, where our energies are painfully drained while losing and
regaining the same positions, advancing and withdrawing the same
flag. There will be constant pressure on language to become "integrated" in itself *and* in all other social activities; the most absurd,
indecent, outlandish verbal and written eruptions will be swallowed
by the general inertia and made into fads, then fashions, then rules.
Words will be tied to things, made subservient to facts, forced to
report about "what is the case." Their ever tenuous physical consistency will be annihilated, their timid presence will go unnoticed,
and they will be made into the transparent, inessential reflection of
something else, something where all the importance lies, something
of which they are but the pale, imperfect, misleading vehicle.
Against all this the philosopher must rebel—*at least* against all this,
given how sterile he is in any other respect. He must wage his war
in the field of language and never underestimate his opponent: never
believe the fight is over, not even after the most outstanding success,

and never believe it will be easy. It will not: the philosopher is also, perhaps, a family man, or a politician, or whatever, the rules of integration and cohesiveness are written in him and in his verbal habits, and he must patiently disengage himself from them, slowly train himself to resist all linguistic training. Which, paradoxically, is a task with its own rules, rules that the philosopher must not only uncover but make his own, make *him*.[12]

First, become aware of how much ordinary, declarative forms of speech support the current, tradition-based, matter-of-fact ideology, to the point of making alternative views inexpressible and inevitably self-refuting. Suppose you want to be nondecisive; suppose you want to suspend conventional practices not because you think some other practices are better, but just to reveal their ultimate unfoundedness, the element of arbitrary choice that lies hidden at their base. How can you even propose to do that, and justify your proposal, without exposing yourself as conceptually confused?

> I can see why the Pyrrhonian philosophers cannot express their general conception in any manner of speaking; for they would need a new language. Ours is wholly formed of affirmative propositions, which to them are utterly repugnant; so that when they say "I doubt," immediately you have them by the throat to make them admit that at least they know and are sure of this fact, that they doubt. (II 12, p. 392)

Second, and in a more constructive vein, shift emphasis away from dangerous declarative statements and use whatever resources language offers to express oneself in a nondeclarative manner: questions, dubitative words, even obscurity. If the opposition—quite naturally—treats these resources as marginal, and as eventually to be resolved in declarations of sorts, you make them central: the trademark of your style.

---

[12] At least these rules will prove effective to undermine a tradition such as that faced by Montaigne. With a different tradition (for example, one initiatied by Montaigne's own work), different rules might be necessary. See the very end of this chapter.

This idea is more firmly grasped in the form of interrogation: "What do I know?"—the words I bear as a motto, inscribed over a pair of scales. (Ibid., p. 393)

We talk about everything didactically and dogmatically. . . . I like these words, which soften and moderate the rashness of our propositions: "perhaps," "to some extent," "some," "they say," "I think," and the like. (III 11, p. 788)

[Aristotle] is the prince of dogmatists; and yet we learn from him that knowing much gives occasion for doubting more. We see him often deliberately covering himself with such thick and inextricable obscurity that we cannot pick out anything of his opinion. It is in fact a Pyrrhonism in an affirmative form. (II 12, p. 376)[13]

Third, do not try to impose the straightjacket of a direction on your vagaries. Definiteness, directionality, and making sense—one, unambiguous sense—may be necessary for pragmatic efficiency in the world of things; but you do not belong to that world, so it is your right and your duty to follow up the wildest associations, the most bizarre occasions for a detour.

Whatever variety of herbs there may be, the whole thing is included under the name of salad. Likewise, . . . I am here going to whip up a hodgepodge of various items. (I 46, p. 201)

Let's go on then, since we are here. (I 48, p. 210)[14]

[13] See also ibid., p. 414: "Aristotle . . . hid beneath a cloud of difficult and unintelligible words and meanings, and left his adherents as much room for debate about his judgment as about the matter itself."

[14] In connection with this exhortation, and with the whole point of this paragraph, it is interesting to consider the remark by Montaigne's secretary that during his travels our author—by his explicit declaration—"was not going anywhere except where he happened to be, and . . . could not miss or go off his path, since he had no plan but to travel in unknown places" (*Travel Journal*, p. 915), as well as Montaigne's justification for continuing the journal himself: "Having dismissed the one of my men who was doing this fine job, and seeing it so far advanced, whatever trouble it may be to me, I must continue it myself" (ibid., p. 947).

Any topic is equally fertile for me. . . . Let me begin with
whatever subject I please, for all subjects are linked with one
another. (III 5, p. 668)

Apropos or malapropos, no matter. (III 11, p. 791)[15]

Fourth, if the opposition rules that you should make ample revi-
sions of all that was written, you will make it a point of revising
nothing at all, of letting contradictions show without taking any
sides—in fact, of *using* contradictions to undermine whatever un-
desired commitment to factuality devolves to you from your being
locked in this rigidly codified, declarative language of ours.

I do not correct my first imaginings by my second—well, yes,
perhaps a word or so, but only to vary, not to delete. (II 37,
p. 574)

I do not portray being: I portray passing. . . . This is a record
of various and changeable occurrences, and of irresolute and,
when it so befalls, contradictory ideas. (III 2, p. 611)

Plato seems to me to have favored this form of philosophizing
in dialogues deliberately, to put more fittingly into diverse
mouths the diversity and variation of his own ideas. (II 12, p.
377)

Fifth, do not restrict this process to one language. Each language
has its limitations; but a lot can be gained, and a lot more can be
expressed, by playing the limitations of one against those of another.

In our language I find plenty of stuff but a little lack of fashioning. . . . And forms of speech, like plants, improve and
grow stronger by being transplanted. (III 5, p. 665)

Let us try to speak this other language [that is, Italian][16] a little.
(*Travel Journal*, p. 990)

[15] See also I 40, p. 186; II 12, p. 341.
[16] About one half of the portion of the *Journal* written by Montaigne (and about
one quarter of the total) is written in Italian.

Sixth, be cautious that your words never be taken as expressing a firm opinion; in fact, if you realize that they are going to be taken that way, refuse to speak.

I do not teach, I tell. (III 2, p. 612)

I care little about the subject matter, opinions are all one to me, and I am almost indifferent about which opinion wins. (III 8, p. 706)

I talk about everything by way of conversation, and about nothing by way of advice. . . . I would not speak so boldly if it were my right to be believed. (III 11, p. 790)

And finally, even when you find yourself at a loss, do not give up your confabulating practice. If verbal language fails you, try other means of expression: "What I cannot express I point to with my finger" (III 9, p. 751).

This is the way to Babel, the way the perplexing "rhapsody"[17] that is Montaigne's book has come about, the book's style—if indeed one "should give the name of style to a formless and undisciplined way of talking, a popular jargon, and a way of proceeding without definitions, without divisions, without conclusions, and confused" (II 17, p. 483). And we can see now that—perverse, formless, and undisciplined as it may be—there is a sense to this operation. One might even say there is a plan, if it were not that *saying* anything is against the plan—at least saying it outright, saying it without taking it back on the next page, without interpolating it with raised eyebrows and question marks, without counterpointing it with, and ultimately burying it in, a bunch of rambling "nonsense." When people got to be too decisive, too united, and too proud, the confusion of tongues proved to be a simple and most effective tactic for stopping them, not by using force but by subtly making them work against one another, by dissipating their energy and ultimately dispersing them.[18] It is the same with the confusion

---

[17] See I 13, p. 32.
[18] See II 12, p. 414: "It was for the chastisement of our pride and the instruction

induced by the philosopher's book: it does not just say things we do
not accept, it says things we do not understand. It does not play by
the rules. It bewilders us, it seems widely off the mark, it seems to
go for another, unknown mark. We might junk it or glance at it
from afar with uneasy curiosity, but either way its author will have
succeeded in carving out for himself a small asylum where language
can be used as a means of liberation and grammar can be violated. It
is not the end of the process, of course: we know that *that* asylum
will soon be conquered. It is part of the game that to end it is to lose
it; so another book will have to follow this one, another small group
of revolutionaries will have to be slowly and patiently trained to
undo all training, to practice taking practices apart, to tell (and
write) what now cannot even be imagined, and thus to draw anew
the confines of imagination.

---

of our wretchedness and incapacity that God produced the disorder and confusion of
the ancient tower of Babel."

CHAPTER EIGHT

KING OF THE HILL

[F]rom [Plutarch and Seneca] I draw like the Danaïds,
incessantly filling up and pouring out. Some of this
sticks to this paper; to myself, little or nothing.
(*I 26, p. 107*)

৵

Probing the Inside

IT HAS BEEN a long and tortuous journey, and we are nearing the
end of it—or at least the point where I will leave off, for the time
being. Thus it may be in order now to retrieve our steps and study
the pattern they drew on the ground: such afterthought may give
us the reassuring sense that we knew where we were going, and that
we got there. In doing this, we will but once again follow the lead
of our guide, who says that the course of our desires and actions

> should be directed not in a straight line that ends up else-
> where, but in a circle whose two extremities by a short sweep
> meet and terminate in ourselves. Actions that are performed
> without this reflexive movement, I mean a searching and gen-
> uine reflexive movement . . . are erroneous and diseased. (III
> 10, p. 773)

I started out by comparing Montaigne's strategy to that of Descartes.[1] Whereas the latter considers the self an existing entity, to be

---

[1] I must insist that, as for the historical Descartes, the position described here is
oversimplified, and that elsewhere I myself have contributed to making it more complex (and more similar to Montaigne's). But I continue to defend the value of such a
simplification, for (at least) the reason given in footnote 13 of Chapter 1.

inspected and searched and then made into the firm, unshakable foundation of finally achieved human wisdom, the former thinks of it as something to be constructed step after step, through commitments in which "one" may find oneself involved by chance, but to which it is forever thereafter bound, until it gradually, through precisely these means, *becomes one*. A central role in this process was assigned to discipline, to that painstaking repetition of moves that only can inscribe a practice in our memory—the memory that matters, the one of muscles and nerves. And then Montaigne's double talk about habit was uncovered: is this most effective determinant of our behavior an indispensable resource to cope with dangers and needs, or a perverse, blinding influence that "robs us of the true appearance of things"—including ourselves? Does it issue in structure or stupidity, in strength or conceit? A conflict of values emerges here, I noted, but whatever side we take, the omnipotence of training will have to be rightly appreciated: even to liberate ourselves from the tyranny of custom we need patient, humble repetition.

At this point in our itinerary, we began to talk less and less of the I and more and more of that soft core of our personality, that "supple," "erratic" agency Montaigne refers to as "mind," "reason," and "imagination." This unruly component was first examined to discover its modes of operation: its concern with nonbeing, with the possible, with the future, its gamelike, joyous experimenting with the unknown, the unheard of, the untried, its affinity with language, the tendency to use ethereal, unsubstantial words—the "airy medium of words" (II 6, p. 274)—as the most common material of its dreams. Then the question was asked what the point of all this playing is, and an answer was found in the uncertainty that haunts us, in the rapid, unpredictable twists of fortune and fate that crush empires and ridicule efficiency: a little craziness now, we resolved, may give us an extra weapon to use when all hell breaks loose and the world goes insane. This answer, on the other hand, does not turn the dedicated ministers of the cult of Reason into the heroes of our story. Theirs is a high-risk venture, in that its outcomes may spread outside the sanctuary before we are ready, or before necessity has made us ready, and cause endless trouble, so we must keep them in there, in isolation, until their time has come. Various ways will be found to disconnect them from actual practices. They will be loaded with a learning that makes their suggestions opaque and virtually useless to most, and with the constitutional guilt of always looking where they are not supposed to and asking the questions they should not ask. And they will be locked into a cage of language, where their revolutions will appear as presumptuous as they are empty, as radical as they are ineffective.

This is as far as we went; now we must ask ourselves whether there is more to this itinerary than casual, implacable free association, the relentless generation of one question after another, or, I should say, of a new question after every answer. Specifically, we must inquire whether the "detour" through the laws and functions of reason—natural as it may have seemed at the time we decided to take it—has taught us anything new on the declared subject of this book: how to search for, or bring about, a self.

Beginning with what is, or sounds, simple, we find in the *Essays* statements such as the following: "Philosophy trains us for ourselves [*nous dresse pour nous*], not for others; for being, not for seeming" (II 37, p. 577). A relatively conventional message is conveyed by these words, indeed one that is surprisingly close to the Cartesian.[2] The outside world is the realm of delusive appearance;[3] there we fragment, and ultimately lose, ourselves by being reflected in the eyes of innumerable spectators, each with his own—limited, biased, misleading—point of view.[4] We must let all those inessential rela-

---

[2] The main difference from a textbook Cartesian account is the decisional (self-prescriptive) element that still remains in this one. See the next paragraph.

[3] See I 46, p. 202 ("it is a base practice, and of very bad consequence in our France, to call everyone by the name of his land and lordship"); II 7, p. 275 ("It was a fine invention . . . to establish certain vain and valueless marks to honor and reward virtue"); III 9, p. 729 ("We do not care so much what we are in ourselves and in reality as what we are in the public mind").

[4] See the interest displayed by Montaigne in the following passage: "I also saw . . . a square box to put jewels in, which contained a certain quantity of them; but since the box was most artfully arranged with mirrors all around, when it was opened it appeared much wider and deeper in every direction, and seemed to hold ten times as many jewels as were in it, since one and the same thing was seen many times by the

tions go and return to the inside, where truth is to be found—or constructed.⁵ "We must reserve a back shop all our own, entirely free, in which to establish our real liberty and our principal retreat and solitude" (I 39, p. 177).⁶ "I do not care so much what I am to others as I care what I am to myself," Montaigne says (II 16, p. 474), and "I am inclined to resist with all my mind these vain externals that delude our judgment through the senses" (III 8, p. 711). "I try to withdraw this corner [that is, my house] from the public tempest, as I do another corner in my soul" (II 15, p. 467), and there "I have set myself no goal but a domestic and private one" (*To the Reader*, p. 2). For this reason, "[i]t is not my deeds that I write down; it is myself, it is my essence" (II 6, p. 274), and even when it comes to reading of the lives of others, he is most interested in writers who "spend more time on plans than on events, more on what comes from within than on what happens without" (II 10, p. 303) because "events are meager evidence of our worth and capacity" (III 8, p. 714), and therefore one is not to "keep a record of [one's] life by [one's] actions . . . [but] by [one's] thoughts" (III 9, p. 721).⁷ Thus "listen: we tell ourselves all we most need" (III 13, p. 822), and "[l]et us leave the people aside . . . who are not conscious of them-

---

reflection of the mirrors, and the mirrors were not easy to detect" (*Travel Journal*, p. 1028).

⁵ See III 13, p. 857: "We seek other conditions because we do not understand the use of our own, and go outside of ourselves because we do not know what it is like inside."

⁶ See also III 9, p. 739, where Montaigne says proudly: "I see no one freer and less indebted than I am up to this point. . . . There is no one who is more absolutely clear of any others."

⁷ See also II 8, p. 291 ("what we engender by the soul, the children of our mind, of our heart and our ability, are produced by a nobler part than the body *and are more our own*" [italics mine]); II 36, p. 573 ("in this respect [of character and conscience] . . . , which alone truly marks what we are"); *Letter* 8, p. 1063 ("punishment and reward . . . concern us directly and as men only by means of honor and shame, inasmuch as these go directly to the soul and are sensed only by the inward feelings *that are most our own*; whereas even the animals are seen to be somewhat susceptible to all other, corporal kinds of reward and punishment" [italics mine]). It is probably for this reason that Montaigne says: "I do not know whether I would not like much better to have produced one perfectly formed child by intercourse with the muses than by intercourse with my wife" (II 8, p. 293).

selves" (II 12, p. 371), since "he who understands nothing about himself, what can he understand?" (ibid., p. 418).

The methodology of this liberation from vain externals is to be the disrespectful countertraining of mind, which patiently educates us to doubt, to negation and blasphemy, to facing without terror the traditional customs' lack of foundation, and to contemplating serenely their many, equally unfounded alternatives. In the void thus created, man might finally begin planning and designing himself, using that will which is the only thing "really in our power" (I 7, p. 20)[8] to become "wholly contained and established within [him]self" (III 2, p. 618) and "master of [him]self in every direction" (III 5, p. 639), thus establishing "[t]rue freedom," which is "to have power over oneself for everything" (III 12, p. 800).

Along these lines, the feat of self-construction becomes an unexpected side effect of the systematic wandering of reason: it is as if by losing the world, the philosopher at least gained himself—more precisely, gained the maneuvering room to pursue the project of a self. The others, well, they have other things to do: they are busy being efficient and adaptive. For them, vain externals may be just the thing: "[D]istinguishing ourselves and our rank externally . . . I truly believe to be very necessary in a state" (I 43, p. 196), and hence "the wise man should withdraw his soul within, out of the crowd, and keep it in freedom and power to judge things freely; but as for externals, he should wholly follow the accepted fashions and forms" (I 23, p. 86). We know why withdrawal is necessary, if indeed looking for oneself is part and parcel of the revolutionary enterprise: we must make sure that we do not "subject public and immutable institutions and observances to the instability of a private fancy (private reason has only a private jurisdiction)" (ibid., p. 88), and that he who "play[s] the fool, . . . [does so] at [his own] expense and without harm to anyone" (II 6, p. 273).

This explanation is simple indeed, perhaps too simple not to be frowned upon. We have learned that Montaigne has good reasons

---

[8] But note that the will "is a very supple and active faculty; it has a lot of agility if we try to immobilize it" (III 5, p. 658).

for disputing straightforward, direct statements, and for favoring obscure, ambiguous ones, so much so that even his repeated claims of naïveté[9] are likely to sound like one more trick, one more way of "pointing with his finger" at what he cannot express. Here is what I believe, the man says, but then he does otherwise, so we are left with the impression that that is what he would *like* (us?) to believe, to get a more reassuring image of himself and his practice—but one that the practice itself, the unsettling practice of probing the inside, will never let be.

Filling the Void

Undoubtedly, the project I sketched sounds sensible. Social functions are roles in a comedy: we must play them to make the whole machine work, but not identify ourselves with them. We must play them "as the part of a borrowed character. Of the mask and appearance we must not make a real essence, nor of what is foreign what is our very own" (III 10, p. 773).[10] On the contrary, we must learn the difficult art of independence: break the net that closes in from all sides, "the violent clutches that engage us elsewhere and draw us away from ourselves" (I 39, p. 178), and develop *our* potentialities, a treasure that, far from being spent, has not even been tapped into yet. "We are each richer than we think, but we are trained to borrow and beg; we are taught to use the resources of others more than our own" (III 12, p. 794).

So far so good. But trouble begins as soon as we try to make the project more specific. Suppose we are no longer conditioned by the rules of custom, we play the social game only as a game or do not play it at all, but in any case we do not think of that game as involving *us*. Now we can address the difficult task of deciding what we are to be. What do we do then? What is our next move?

The problem is: we have already established that we "are nothing

---

[9] See I 39, p. 181; III 5, p. 640; III 13, p. 822.
[10] At I 26, p. 131, Montaigne says that he "was considered a master craftsman" in acting.

but ceremony" (II 17, p. 478), and that it is only by long usage that this "form" turns into "substance." Of course, we have the *idea* of a *truer* substance, one that remains identical with itself through many misleading manifestations, but that idea can only be counted now as a delusive myth. The Cartesian may have a right to use it, at least to give direction to his search, but we have already decided that there is nothing to find—not in us, in any case—unless we bring it about, and that bringing it about means praying until faith comes,[11] exercising until our muscles respond automatically. Our only hope of making ourselves real is to espouse form, some form, to the end, and start the double recursion of habit; then we might develop an "ability" that is truly "within" us, not "external and fortuitous" (*Letter* 5, p. 1060). But how can this process be initiated if all we practice is opposing one form to another, convincing ourselves of their optional character, and thus ultimately destroying confidence? Isn't it the case that this behavior, in principle, can only *make* a void, not *fill* it?

There is an analogy between this situation and that of a king, at least as Montaigne had experience of the latter.[12] A king of Montaigne's time was an absolute monarch, where the original meaning of the word "absolute" (Latin: *absolutus*) is "set free, disconnected, untied." An absolute king is not bound by the rules of society, in a way he is not even part of society: this is how he can *make* rules and establish policy. Whereas everybody else is *relative* to his many social tasks and defines himself variously through them, the king is entirely self-enclosed and self-standing, independent, apart:

> No one follows [the king] for any friendship there may be between [the two]; for no friendship can be knit where is so little relation and correspondence. [The king's] elevation has placed [him] outside of human association: there is too much disparity and disproportion. (I 42, p. 195)[13]

[11] See I 56, pp. 230-31: "We pray out of habit and custom. . . . All in all, [praying] is only an act."

[12] At III 8, p. 720, Montaigne says: "I . . . am king of the matter I treat" (and remember, that matter is himself).

[13] See also III 7, p. 701: "[The king's] fortune repels society and companionship."

This also means that the king will have to face the same emptiness the self does, after cutting all knots and setting up to give himself an absolute reality, unrelated to anything else. "It takes so much to be a king that he exists only as such," Montaigne says (III 7, p. 702),[14] and we begin to wonder whether the same might be true of the project of subjectivity, whether by developing that complete dominion and mastery of ourselves which is only possible when nothing else is at stake we might end up like the ruler unruled, who "has nothing that is properly his own . . . [and] owes his very self to others" (III 6, p. 689).

That there is something to this suspicion, the following passage reveals:

> I have an aping and imitative nature. When I used to dabble in composing verse . . . , it clearly revealed the poet I had last been reading. . . . In Paris I speak a language somewhat different than at Montaigne. Anyone I regard with attention easily imprints on me something of himself. What I consider, I usurp: a foolish countenance, an unpleasant grimace, a ridiculous way of speaking. (III 5, p. 667)[15]

Note that such aping is entirely functional to the "spread" promoted by the mind. Remember some of the tactical hints thrown at us by the Pyrrhonian reformer of language: associate freely, try the most disparate points of view and means of expression, never think you are going anywhere except where you happen to be. But all of a sudden, this strategy has become a problem, insofar as we can no longer see it as a preliminary step that clears the ground before building begins. Left to ourselves, without the solid if irrational support of custom, we can build nothing at all. We used aping against aping, aping as a deconstructive tool against the aping that comes from our mysterious ancestry, and now all we are left with is aping for its own sake, aping run wild. We tried to silence the many voices that spoke confusedly around us, and all we find

---

[14] See also ibid., p. 700: "The toughest and most difficult occupation in the world, in my opinion, is to play the part of a king worthily."

[15] See also I 21, p. 68: "I catch the disease that I study, and lodge it in me."

now, "inside," are more of the same voices speaking even more confusedly:

> All contradictions may be found in me by some twist and in some fashion. Bashful, insolent; chaste, lascivious; talkative, taciturn; tough, delicate; clever, stupid; surly, affable; lying, truthful; learned, ignorant; liberal, miserly, and prodigal: all this I see in myself to some extent according to how I turn; and whoever studies himself really attentively finds in himself, yes, even in his judgment, this gyration and discord. (II 1, p. 242)

Not that the confusion will not be resisted. Our intention is "not [to] speak the minds of others except to speak [our] own mind[s] better" (I 26, p. 108), that is, to use others as tools to confirm our opinions, not as stamps to imprint us with foreign wisdom. We are inclined to think that some judgments and ideas are natural to us, and that what others can give us is only "a firmer grip" on them (II 17, p. 499), a better articulation of the relevant arguments and conclusions.

> I have studied . . . not at all to form my opinions, but certainly to assist, second, and serve those which I formed long ago. (II 18, p. 505)

> [I]n things where I have only my judgment to employ, other people's reasons can serve to support me, but seldom to change my course. (III 2, p. 618)

> Plutarch . . . will reveal to you my views . . . much better than I could myself. (*Letter* 9, p. 1066)

Following this inclination, it would be reasonable to trust our prejudices and accept the words of others when, and only when, they "feel" right. But is the inclination itself reasonable? How do we know that those prejudices are indeed "natural" to us? Couldn't they simply come from older readings? Isn't it true that "[w]hat I retain of [books] is something I no longer recognize as anyone else's" (II 17, p. 494)?[16]

Perhaps we should leave thoughts and words aside to find something that is truly our own. Didn't we say that the way we move and act and react is the way we are? Well, then, let us systematically observe our behavior and "record those [habits] that [we] have seen most frequently in action" (III 13, p. 827): they will give us the starting point, and then we will be free to add and enrich and elaborate with all the resources of language and learning. Let us spy on our behavior as from an external vantage point, "surprise" ourselves in our "ordinary actions" (II 29, p. 533); if we can do it with others, to "reveal . . . , by their outward manifestations, their inward inclinations" (III 13, p. 824), perhaps we can do it with ourselves, too.[17]

But it will not work. What would we be observing then if not the residue of reform, the limit of our courage, the evidence of our misery and finitude? It may be "too late to become other than I am" (III 10, p. 772), but only because I am old and tired, and such weaknesses are not a promising way to begin the articulation of a self. Do we want to cluster our being around the battles we could not fight, the steps we were afraid to take, the rites we timidly held to? Doesn't this reduce our case to that of the unconscious, unreflective, efficient brutes who could not care less for mind or revolution— indeed, even a bad copy of that, given how much *less* efficient and more troubled we are? Should we conclude that our digression through the workings of reason told us nothing about the ways of the self, and that these ways can be trodden only by those who would rather be stupid than mad?

We are in a quandary. It seems that, if "no man has arrived at himself" (III 12, p. 799), it is because he can't. Either he unquestioningly follows ancient rules and then develops a consistency of reactions and moves that might convince an *outside* viewer that he is but one entity, that he systematically pursues a consistent set of in-

---

[16] See also III 12, p. 809: "I, among so many borrowings of mine, am very glad to be able to hide one now and then."

[17] In fact, in the last passage quoted Montaigne claims that it is precisely by doing this detective work with himself that he has learned to do it with others.

tentions, but he will hardly be aware of it, in fact, he will hardly be aware of anything: for him, awareness is an unnecessary, annoying distraction, and forethought is a luxury for the rich and lazy.[18] Or he tries to detach himself from the old ways and find something that is more truly his own, but then there will be nothing to find: any choice will be as arbitrary as any other, any voice will echo innumerable other voices. More likely than not, few or none of us are pure cases of either alternative. In general, we oscillate between them: forget ourselves at times—the *issue* of ourselves—and wonder about our "inner nature" at other times, only to be stupefied at seeing how slippery and paradoxical that is. There may be a point to this oscillation, as we have seen: a point whose scope is well beyond us, in the grand laws of how our species is to maintain its delicate adaptive equilibrium. But those who worry about subjectivity will not be satisfied with hearing only of this general point; they will want to know something more specific about the role of the "inside" and of the self. Are these just *any* delusions, designed by astute nature to keep us endlessly drifting and deviating, or is there a rationale to the choice, a logic to this empty pursuit of an inexistent center of force?

The Discipline of Displacement

To put it plainly, my answer to the last question, and my farewell as this book comes to an end, is the following. There is no *thing* to be found or constructed inside. A thing is a coherent conglomerate, it shows syntonic, directional behavior; so to make a thing is to forget what could be instead, and to concentrate on what is in front of

[18] Given the reversal of values and priorities promoted here concerning theories and practices (for which see footnote 26 of Chapter 6 and the attending text), the stories told to convince ourselves and others that what we do is what we intend to do to realize some goals must be conceived as a posteriori rationalizations of what has happened (or, we know, will happen) anyway—that is, as instances of the intellectual practice of rationalizing. ("[T]here is nothing like divining about things past," says Montaigne at II 30, p. 539.) And those who are busy with other, more directly useful practices may be impatient with tales of this kind.

us, and how best to make it stand on its feet. But the tools by which we look inside are inadequate to this task: they are tools for taking apart, for analyzing, for throwing whatever falls into their scope against an array of unactualized possibilities and absurd dreams. Therefore, if the self is to be a thing, then there is no self; if inside is to be a place, that place is empty. There is only one place, and one kind of thing: the *spatio*-temporal world. And there is only one way of becoming one—that of steadily pursuing continuity and conformism: "The recommendation everyone seeks for liveliness and promptness of wit, I aspire to for orderliness; what they seek for a brilliant and signal deed, or for some particular ability, I aspire to for order, consistency, and tranquillity of opinions and conduct" (II 17, p. 499). [19] For those who would refuse this conventional wisdom and lend ear to the sirens of imagination, the conclusion is desolating, if not dangerous.

> I have no other marshal but fortune to arrange my bits. As my fancies present themselves, I pile them up; now they come pressing in a crowd, now dragging single file. . . . I let myself go as I am. Besides, these are not matters of which we are forbidden to be ignorant and to speak casually and at random. (II 10, p. 297)

On the other hand, to say that the inside is empty is not to say that *looking inside* is pointless. Looking inside is not looking at a thing: it is looking *away from things*, at what is not a thing (yet?). And since things are constituted in the middle of practices, as their relatively stable referents, and practices are social, public affairs— repeatable behavioral sequences that belong to no one in particular and could in principle be performed by all—the invention of an *in-*

[19] At II 2, p. 245, speaking of drunkenness, Montaigne says: "The worst condition of man is when he loses knowledge and control of himself." But his conflicting values surface once more in same essay, when he says things like: "[W]e should make our daily drinking habits more expansive and vigorous. . . . [W]e should refuse no chance to drink, and have this desire always in our head. . . . [D]runkenness to Plato is a good and certain test of each and every man's nature, and at the same time suited to give older people the courage to make merry in dances and music, useful pastimes that they shy away from in a sober mood" (pp. 247, 249).

side that is by definition nonsocial and that automatically sets up its correlative *outside* as the category to which every *thing* is to belong, intimates that everything is not all that matters,[20] that there are alternatives to it. These alternatives will have to be explored in solitude and spoken to no audience, for "[s]ociety in general can do without our thoughts": we must give it "the rest—our actions, our work, our fortunes, and our very life" (I 23, p. 86), and only then it will leave us in peace. Some might ask "what is left?" and they will be but widely missing the point. No *thing* is left, nothing but negation and non-being, nothing but silence and soliloquy, nothing but ultimate privacy, the privacy perhaps of one's own death: "Dying is not a role for society; it is an act for one single character" (III 9, p. 748).

In the end, this is what is at issue in the project of a self. A self is unique, a self is apart, a self is "in" us, and nothing in the world of things is like that. Everything calls upon the Other, requires the Other for its very definition; everything belongs to a *kind*. In the world, things are outside, side-by-side one another: the ultimate law of coexistence is impenetrability, taking space and excluding all else from it. So looking inside is not looking for one more pebble; it is looking for an article of a different brand, and it is also looking in a different way. If we describe it as looking at all, it is because our language is poor and bent to the social ways, the ways of (outside) things. What we have here is an effort, a striving, but not properly a looking: not a looking *at*, not a looking *for*. All these activities have an object. In fact, all activities are supposed to have an object or they would be pointless: so recites the tradition. But we want to rebel against tradition, we want to use its own words against it, so we will talk of a looking that is not a looking, of a construction that is in fact a destruction, of a place that is displaced. Our major weapon in this struggle will be the erection of a category that is alternative to all that was there before, and to which we will assign a dignity equal to that of all that was there before: the category of a

---

[20] In Chapter 3 of *Kant's Copernican Revolution*, I discuss the way in which such apparently absurd claims result from trying to stretch a language away from its conceptual framework.

reality into which we will retreat, and from whose point of view we will not be afraid to judge, and condemn, and ridicule, the opposition.

Is this "the death of the subject?" In a way, yes, but in a trivial way. It is because we discovered that the ways of the subject are the ways of death, of what "others" could only regard as death. But it is not in the sense that there is no subtracting from the cosmic importance of the subject, from the turn it inaugurates in our experience. The position of the subject is the ultimate—and the primary—revolutionary move: it is contesting the legitimacy of history, the accountability of tradition, the foundedness of truth. It is calling in question, opening the can of worms, yelling that the king has no clothes. And it is doing all this even though—indeed, *because*—it won't matter: not to introduce a new factor into the world of things, not to acquire more power there, and not even to understand it better, because you won't.[21] It is doing it as something separate, something that calls for its own justification and its own rules, a task that is irrelevant to all but what happens *inside*: "[The mind] can see and feel all things, but it should feed only on itself, and should be instructed about what properly concerns it and what is properly of its own possession and its own substance" (III 10, p. 771).[22]

Those who talk of the death of the subject are the last Cartesians. They look for something, they don't find it, and they conclude that there is nothing there: not to the object of the search, and not to the search itself. My answer to them—as I found it in Montaigne's book—comes in two stages. First, there are things you cannot find because their being requires your effort:[23] you must *do* something

[21] For remember: "You will find there is nothing so insipid in all the dishes on your table as this fine entertainment of [a man's] mind . . . ; and you will find that his ideas and aspirations are not worth your stew" (III 13, p. 856).

[22] Ultimately, it is this separateness, this revolutionary positing of an inside, that is responsible for the "distinction between mind and body" and for all the attending "problems." This means that such a distinction is to be conceived as an act—an act of negation and challenge, a political act—and as one that cannot be performed once and for all but must be repeated over and over again, every time "the public" appropriates the counterfactual absurdities dreamt "inside."

[23] In fact, this is probably true of all things, if we are to believe Kant's doctrine of synthesis. See *Kant's Copernican Revolution* and Chapter 1 above.

before they come to life, and not do it just once, but do it until it becomes natural, until the effort no longer shows. Second, the same holds true not only of things but also of what our language has no name for: that alternative to things, that negation of things, which is hinted at, if only vaguely, by the expression "inside." This inside requires our work, our constant work of detaching ourselves from what happens and what is done, of blaming its falsity, its triviality, its misery—that is, its incapacity to include all truths, all claims, all views. The moment we stop working, we are left with a "dead and mute portrait" (II 37, p. 596), with "a cadaver on which the veins, the muscles, and the tendons appear at a glance, each part in its place" (II 6, p. 274), and at one point we will have to stop, since our time is not infinite.[24] But until then we must leave room in our life, and in our society, for this destabilizing practice, for this guilt-ridden rejection of public beliefs and values, for this coming away from the crowd and relentlessly, madly challenging its wisdom. And we must do it right, by words, perhaps, if that hurts less, but not by words that are only announced: by words that usage makes familiar, and that slowly displace us, disengage us, disconnect us from all that was familiar before—for the time being at least, the time it takes for us to become blind to *them* and to be in need of still newer provocations. It may well turn out to be in the interest of that very crowd, when the nightmares entertained "inside," in the place of solitude and shame, decide to go public and become part of the world.

[24] In this connection, it is interesting to note that such a "dead and mute portrait" is exactly what Montaigne draws in the last essay, while he passes on to others the endless task of probing the inside.

BIBLIOGRAPHY

Bencivenga, Ermanno. "Descartes, Dreaming, and Professor Wilson." *Journal of the History of Philosophy* 21 (1983), pp. 75–85.

———. *Kant's Copernican Revolution*. New York: Oxford University Press, 1987.

———. "A New Paradigm of Meaning." *Synthese* 73 (1987), pp. 599–621. Reprinted in *Looser Ends*.

———. "Philosophy One and Two." *Nous* 21 (1987), pp. 161–78. Reprinted in *Looser Ends*.

———. "Theories and Practices." *The Monist* 70 (1987), pp. 212–22. Reprinted in *Looser Ends*.

———. *Looser Ends*. Minneapolis: University of Minnesota Press, 1989.

Frege, Gottlob. "Thoughts." Translated by Peter Geach and R. H. Stoothoff. In *Collected Papers on Mathematics, Logic, and Philosophy*, edited by Brian McGuinness, pp. 351–72. (Oxford: Basil Blackwell, 1984).

Kant, Immanuel. *Critique of Pure Reason*. Translated by Norman Kemp Smith. New York: St. Martin Press, 1965.

INDEX